WHITE BOY IN THE COLORED SECTION

Finding Myself By Finding Others

DEDICATION:

Endless thanks to Louise, Lula, George, Eli, and so many others for their kind example of faith in the midst of turmoil. Special appreciation to Laurel Johnson, Elena Johnson, and Anthony Wilson for encouraging me to compose these accounts in the first place. Heartfelt gratitude to SaraEllen for listening and guiding in her soft, wise way.

PROLOGUE:

A young, naïve white boy in the early 1960's unknowingly sat in the wrong hospital waiting room, the "Colored Waiting Room," creating a disorder that stirred his soul, and set him on a lifelong course of striving to grasp the culture of segregation and prejudice in which he lived—forever struggling to fulfill his small role of helping the nightmare resolve.

(Photo: US Government Public Domain Images)

FOREWORD:

I was born in Athens, Georgia in 1952. We soon after moved to the almost exclusively white region of North Georgia. For the first 8 years of my life, I had no awareness of other races or racial differences. I had lived all those years absent any natural bias, bigotry, or racism. Racism has to be learned.

Some of my dearest black friends encouraged me to write these accounts of my passage from unbiased innocence to racial turmoil and eventually social resolution. Some of the events herein will astound the reader. Some may prove shocking or repugnant. But there is much to be learned hereby. Please take a look into my life as a naïve white boy in the days of overpowering racial discrimination, and the many phases of painful progress I lived through. I plead that black folks will forgive my expression of pain, for theirs was the greater. But we have come through it together. Where are we now?

SPECIAL NOTE:

In the days of my youth, the term "colored people" was considered polite. It was also the term used by most black folks where I lived. "Negro" was accepted in journalism and within formal addresses. "Black" was seldom heard. No hurtful or degrading terms will be used herein, except where absolutely necessary to illustrate a higher point; and even so, will not be spelled out completely.

~ *The Author*

PART 1: SWEET INNOCENCE OF YOUTH

1952:

I was born while my parents were at the University of Georgia. We lived in married student housing. Thus my first home was on the UGA campus, and I have been a Bulldog fan since birth; (a fact I was proud to relate to Coach Vince Dooley when I met him years later.) Despite UGA being a state university, by rule there were no black students accepted there until 1961.

Sometime afterward my mother took employment while my father completed his studies. They hired a black girl named Sammie Lee to watch me. I do not remember her, or any black people from that period, since we moved when I was two and a half. But my parents always told me that I loved Sammie Lee dearly; whenever we would drive through Athens, upon seeing any black girl her age I would call out, "Sammie Lee! Sammie Lee!" There was a definite and natural bond between this white toddler and his black babysitter.

1957:

Now I was age five, and was entirely unaware that there were black people in the world. I remember watching quite a lot of television programs, but do not recall ever seeing any black people on the screen. We were living in Hiawassee, Georgia in the Appalachian Mountains, and there were likewise no blacks near us. I had never heard of them; they weren't even allowed to enter our remote Appalachian world through the vast cross-cultural communication modality of television. Then one day my five-year-old world turned: My mother was driving us kids to go shopping over the line in Hayesville, North Carolina. I saw a man walking along the highway who was—colored! I spun around in my seat and called out to my big brother, "Martin! What kind of man is that?"

"A colored man," he replied.

"How did he get colored?" My eyes were wide and my mouth hung open in awe.

"God made some people white, and some people colored. You know how we see Indians in the movies, who are red? Well, colored people are colored black."

"Mama! I just saw a colored man!" I spun around in my seat toward her so fast, I practically slung my words at the back of her head. "God made him a different color than us!" Lacking any memory of Sammie Lee or other blacks in Athens, I had no reference point upon which to base my new discovery.

Mama drove steadily on, nodded a little, and never answered. I was confused that she was not astonished as I was. It was like the first time I saw pink clouds as a three year old, and despite my excited announcement, I could not get any of the grownups to even look or act impressed at my astounding discovery. Or like the guy in the sci-fi film who is the only one to see the flying saucer, and no one else is interested. Spellbound, I kept looking back down the highway until the figure disappeared. He dressed like us, he walked like us, he had a face like us. He was a person like us. I thought about it a long while.

1958:

By the time I was six, we had made enough trips to North Carolina that I had seen several colored people of all ages. They were still not part of my world. I would observe them intently for a few brief moments as our car passed them by, leaving them behind us in their world as we propelled forward in ours, separated by glass and steel and unseen social barriers. Then in the summer we made a trip to Washington, DC. I was impressed at how many black people lived there; they were a regular part of the scene—a routine scene, yet entirely novel to me. Still, they seemed to drift by in steady currents of their own humanity, among us but apart from us. Crystal clear in my mind today remains the image of the tall, black gentleman in his fine suit and fedora, just as my Dad would attire himself; and ladies in dresses as neat and well appointed as white women wore. They were so different and somehow so alike, I pondered on it a long time. These were just people.

"Mama. Daddy. Why are there so many colored people in this place?" I queried. Mama's reply was a sudden but silent *Shhsh!* (I was later to learn that white people did not talk about colored people, especially when they are around.)

I do not recall seeing any blacks near the national monuments in Washington, nor the Capitol, nor any place being frequented by the many white tourists and government and business people. Then as we walked through a park, we met what seemed like hundreds of black folk, busily on their way. Mama was holding my little brother Stephen, age four, when he called out, "Mama! Just look at all those colored people!" My parents looked stupefied. A few of the people glanced toward us, but they all kept passing by, unaffected. But what a fascinating novelty this was. I had lived eight years and still had never spoken with, nor interacted with, a black person except as an infant.

1960:

We moved across the state to Rome, Georgia when I was eight. I began to see more black people, and would observe them from our car. What were they like? How did they live? They seemed to be going about the same things we generally were: shopping, working, commuting. But more of them walked or rode the city bus than actually drove. Why, I had never even seen a city bus, having lived in such a rural place until now. Rome was like a big city to me, and I marveled at its sites everywhere we went.

I had never thought about the concept of blacks being in the same public schools as whites, since we had no blacks in Hiawassee. But in my new school I saw there were no blacks either, despite there being a strong presence of them in Rome.

I asked Mama, "Where are all the colored kids, at school time? I see colored kids in Rome, but never at school."

I knew my Mama knew everything about everything, and she would be able to give me the correct answer. But it was not the answer I expected. "They don't go to the same schools as white kids," she replied.

"But why?" The concept was so alien to my young and innocent mind, I felt my head whirring in a mildly anxious state of confusion. "Don't they learn just like us? Or are they supposed to learn different things? What is it about them that they can't come to my school?"

"They're not supposed to. They're not allowed to go any place with white people."

I sat in numb silence; then as we passed a large place of worship I queried further, "Not even church?"

Mama thought a moment, then answered, "You won't see them at any white churches, or any whites at their churches. That's just the way people are. They like to be with their own kind."

"But if they wanted to go to a—a *white* church. Could they?"

"They know it would stir up trouble with some of the meaner ones, who don't want to be around them. It wouldn't work out."

"But we have the same God, don't we? I think if a church is mean to anyone, it is not really God's church."

My response clearly made Mama nervous. But after another couple of blocks she eventually gave me a reassuring pat on the knee and said, "You are a good boy. Just pray for everybody. Everybody is loved by God." I felt such a relief upon hearing Mama's affirmation that black people were worthy in God's eyes; I suspected as much. But my anxiety tried to worm its way back in when she continued, "Just don't be talking about things like this with people. It will make them upset." I could see I had a lot of praying to do, for my own worries if for nothing else.

Another day soon after, we drove past a laundromat. A sign on the window said "Whites Only." I asked Mama, "Why do they only let you wash white clothes there?" *Ah, sweet innocence of youth.*

Mama looked startled. I was asking *"colored folk" questions* again. She managed to coolly answer, "Well, actually, that means that only white people can go in there."

"Huh? Why?"

"It's like the schools and everything else. White people—some white people—don't want colored people in their places of business. If they let them in, the white customers would quit coming." Mama paused and reflected, then went on. "They have their own neighborhoods, their own restaurants, and even their own movie theaters."

I had to gnaw on that one awhile. I saw blacks walking down the sidewalk, and wondered how they felt from not being able to go into that laundromat. Gradually having the shell of segregation opened to me had made me feel like I had walked into a horror movie, but now that it was gaping open, the movie began to envelope me and I was part of the horror. There was no exit door; I had to deal with this deep in my soul.

There were no black people in our neighborhood. They all lived clear across town, mostly in dismal housing projects. The only ones we saw were road workers patching our street, or those working on the garbage trucks. No whites worked on the garbage trucks. Stephen and I would stop and observe them from our front yard, or while walking to school, silently analyzing them as they compared to us. They didn't speak much, so we couldn't gather an abundance of insights from their conversational style. They were very serious and well behaved, and paid close attention to their work. But they worked in a world of their own.

1961:

Stephen and I were playing in the yard when a big green truck came up the street. Black men were patching potholes on Brookwood Avenue in West Rome. Three workers walked behind the truck. The foreman would blow a whistle for the truck to stop. One man would spray tar into the hole from a nozzle, another would shovel gravel into it and hit it a lick or two, then the hose man would spray it once more. The foreman would blow his whistle again, and the truck would move forward. Stephen ran in the house and got his toy whistle, then hid in the bushes and watched. Soon as the tar started to spray, Stephen blew his whistle and the truck lunged forward prematurely, causing hot tar to spew onto the men's shoes. The men, startled at first, barely glanced toward Stephen. The men called out for the truck to stop, then went on with their work. I later learned that the men knew they could never retaliate against or even scold a six year old white child. But the cool, internal self-control they exhibited was more valorous than any brave deed I had ever witnessed; and was equal to any racial fear they may have harbored.

We were embarrassed for them, and lay concealed in the bushes until they were gone. Later we told a neighbor boy and he got a laugh out of it. He told his mother who told ours, and we got a lecture on human kindness which I never forgot.

"Just think about how poor they are," Mama whined with empathy. "They can't even get onto a white boy—but I sure can. And I will! Be nice to everybody. God made us all!"

Then there was Louise. Mama returned to work and she and Daddy hired a black woman to keep house, and to tend my baby sisters while my brothers and I were at school. Mama prepared me for Louise: "She is a very nice colored lady. She will be good to you. Be sure and be very polite to her. Mind her, and help her when she needs you to." It was an important first lesson for me: *be polite to her.* It cheered my heart to learn that a colored person was equally deserving of—and in need of—human courtesy.

Then one afternoon she was there, just as I walked in the house from school. She was an attractive young woman about thirty, wearing a white uniform dress. Stephen and I had come in running and laughing, then suddenly we were perfect little mannequins of behavior as we inched across the floor. She was ironing in the kitchen and I had to squeeze past her to get to my room. She and I both said "Excuse me." Her tone was gentle and sincere. I had just had my first verbal exchange with a black person!

WHITE BOY IN THE COLORED SECTION

"Which one are you?" she asked with a smile. I turned around and said, "Joe."

Then she pointed and said, "Then you must be Stephen." "Yes ma'am," we both replied.

"Well, I'm Louise, and I'm so glad to meet you," she responded, her narrow face moving slightly side to side as if to convey interest in us, or to push her words along with symbolic goodwill. "Your Mama wants you to get right on your homework." More emphasis with the twisting of her head. "Then you can have a snack."

"Yes ma'am."

Her complexion contrasted noticeably with her white uniform dress. I wondered why she did not wear a brown or black dress. She looked very nice and professional, almost making me think of nurses. I wondered if there were black nurses, and if they wore brown or black uniforms; or if they wore white ones, to make white people happy—to conform to the white world. She stayed busy at her duties as we observed her keenly from the corners of our eyes. When our parents got home, Mama drove her the quarter-mile to the bus stop. The evening was like any other. There was no discussion about this novel presence in our midst. Louise was like a visiting ghost; not yet tangible, but destined to play a major role in my youthful development.

There was an excellent Boys' Club in the neighborhood, and my brothers and I were soon privileged to be members. We enjoyed games, sports, crafts, a reading room, and good fellowship. One time some of the boys organized a touch-football game out on the field. We needed a couple more boys. Outside the fence walked two black boys. "Come in and play with us," one of the white boys called out. The black boys kept walking. Then several of us repeated the request, "C'mon in and play football with us."

One of the boys replied, "We can't go in there. It just for white folks." I stared blankly, embarrassed for those boys' sakes. The street outside the fence was lined with houses where blacks resided, yet they could not enter the Boys' Club which they could see every day from their front porches. Sometimes we would have large sporting events, especially football and baseball, with bleachers full of spectators. Yet the black boys could only watch from outside the fence.

One afternoon two black boys came to the gate and attempted to pay admission to watch a game, but were turned away with the phrase, "Sorry, no colored." My senses would always grow numb at the thought of how such occurrences must make them feel, as if they were subhuman. Could a lashing with a rawhide whip hurt any worse? Probably not in the long run.

Routinely I began to observe the force that maintains the spirit of segregation, like a living being that permeates all of society. For instance, Boys Club staff may come to work and say to some black youth outside, "How ya boys doing?", then walk on past them to the entrance, knowing they could not come in. If a black boy came over and peered in through the glass door to see the white boys having fun, a staff member would open the door and say, "You boys need to run along now." Even kindhearted whites knew the subtle and ever-dominant rules of segregation. It was not only bodily segregation, but segregation of mind and soul as well. Social segregation—civilization advancing for whites, while blacks were left in the dust of progress.

In town I began to see separate drinking fountains in public buildings, labeled White and Colored. Places of business usually only had one fountain, if any at all, and would not segregate them because blacks would not enter most white establishments. They would enter white-owned grocery stores, but there was were no drinking fountains in stores.

I recall being in a grocery store with Mama. I began to pull returned soda bottles from their crates, turning them up to sip the dregs from them. Mama was shocked on turning around to observe my boorish behavior, and quietly snapped at me, "That's nasty! Colored people might have drunken from those bottles!" I must have looked aghast, as I quickly returned my last bottle to the rack and wiped my mouth on my sleeve. That was my natural reaction, which actually surprised and embarrassed me moments later. I was inculcating the white attitude toward blacks.

But then I had to think: what made black people nastier than us? All she needed to say was, *people* have had their mouths on those bottles. And flies have inhabited them. And all manner of filth has surely come across them. Any of those admonitions would have thwarted any further attempt on my part to glean a few free drops of soda. So here was my kindly mother, who was always so considerate of black people, reminding me of a keystone in our societal relationship with blacks: be kind to them, but keep them in their place; and keep them at a distance. Even the most kindhearted white people had that little windmill ever spinning in their minds. It was a social mindset that pervaded white thought, even subconsciously. And though racial tension in general was nothing compared to the Civil War days, nevertheless here we were, a century later, as total segregation prevailed in the days of jet air travel, television, and the beginnings of the space program.

I continued to observe Louise with the keenest interest. I was fascinated with ways she was different from us, but also ways she was the same. When summer vacation came, I was with her all day. She had the duty of informing us of our chores, supervising us occasionally to see that our playtime led to nothing disastrous, making our lunch, and occasionally rescuing us from bicycle wrecks or whenever we got stuck in a tree. She got to be like a big sister or an aunt to us, and we got along fine. Still, there was no in-depth conversation about life, or her life. She did mention her kids once in a while, such as how she wore them out with a switch when they pulled some of the stunts we pulled. And she did have permission to use a switch on us!

One day she went out to a shrub and broke off a switch, and left it standing on the kitchen counter where we could see it. She warned us that we were getting out of line, and she had a switch at the ready, just in case we needed our legs stung. Eventually Stephen pulled some raucous caper, as boys do, which warranted a whipping. Afterward, six year old Stephen scowled at her and loudly declared, "Louise! You're fired!" I was embarrassed for her sake, but she just laughed it off. That was the moment I realized she was as much a human as we, and, at least in our home, held just as much authority over us as any adult would have, white or not. Within our little microcosmic world, she held authority over us, at least from 8:00 to 4:00. Then she returned to her own world of inferior co-existence.

She was too smart to pull tricks on, or to manipulate into giving us access to treats Mama had put up out of our reach. She did a fair job of keeping us in line. But she was fair and kind, and cooed over our little sisters Laura and Liz. We came to trust and love Louise, and could always rely on her for security.

Louise let us watch a reasonable amount of television, particularly in the morning and afternoon when most of the kids' shows were on. But she had us go outside and play when "her shows" came on, particularly soap operas and occasionally a game show. Sometimes I would watch them with her, and if she had a day off, I would update her the next day on what happened to so-and-so on her favorite soap, "The Secret Storm." She had no TV at home. I would feel like such a big shot, greatly impressing an adult with the details of the latest carryings-on of the characters.

One day we got a particularly entertaining treat. While we were outside, we heard some interesting music on our radio in the kitchen. I sneaked inside and peeked around the doorway. While doing the ironing she was twisting and grooving to the coolest music on some magical, unknown radio station we had never listened to before. It was Soul and Rhythm-n-Blues. I slipped back outside and told the kids and friends that Louise was dancing with the ironing board! We took turns climbing atop the garbage can to peer in through the kitchen window at the fascinating spectacle. I could have charged admission. It marked the beginning of my interest in Blues.

Another time the TV was on during the news broadcast. Louise had gone to the kitchen to prepare lunch. I was just passing through the den and overheard the announcer say something I thought disgusting. I went straight to Louise and told on him, "That man on TV said something bad about colored people!"

"What did he say?" Her response came with controlled interest, but clear focus, as she awaited my explanation.

"He said two n_______rs were arrested! My Mama and Daddy said that is a bad word to call colored people!"

Calm as ever, she softly replied, "He probably said *negro*. That's a polite word. It's okay."

This was the first time I ever mentioned race to a black person, and it would be years before the situation arose again. It generally was not done in those days, and if so, would generate uncomfortable feelings for both parties. But Louise was cool about it. At any rate, I could not wait to show off my new knowledge to big brother Martin. Soon as he came home, I went back to his bedroom and told him, "Louise taught me a polite word to call colored people. It's n_______r-o."

Martin was stunned. Half smiling at my *faux pas*, half scowling at my uncalled-for display of ignorance, he was quick to sternly correct me: "The word is *negro*; not what *you* said! It's best to just not say that word, and just say colored people. You won't get in any trouble that way."

"What kind of trouble?"

"Colored people get embarrassed if you talk about them being something different from us. And white people get upset if you talk about colored people at all. And you never hear the word negro except on the news, mostly. Or in the newspaper, or history books."

"Is that why a boy got in trouble at school the other day? He walked into class and said he saw two colored boys on the way to school. The teacher told him to be quiet and sit down."

"It's not polite to talk about them. Ever. You can be polite to them, but it's not polite to talk about them."

"But they're not all bad. Louise is not bad."

"It's just the mess everything is in. They got free from slavery, but they just didn't ever get to be Americans. Nobody likes to talk about it."

I was beginning to learn the niceties and taboos of race relations at a steady pace. But the biggest surprise of my young life was soon to occur. Little Liz had cut her finger on a can lid one evening, and Mama was taking her to the hospital for some sutures. She had me come along to sit by her, and comfort her during the drive. When we arrived, Mama told me to just take a seat in the waiting room.

Now here was a puzzle. There were two alcoves filled with benches. One had a sign reading "White Waiting Room," and the other "Colored Waiting Room." I honestly did not know what this meant. I did not know what qualified a person to sit in either area. I saw hospital staff in white uniforms, then some in colored scrub uniforms. Then there were the volunteer girls, the Candy Stripers, with their white and red striped skirts, whose uniforms were both white and colored. There being no one in the white waiting room left no clues as to where I was supposed to sit. Everything in the hospital seemed to follow a stern protocol, so I figured people in colored clothes were to sit in the colored waiting room.

Since I was wearing colored clothes, I sauntered over to the colored waiting room and took a seat on the front row. An elderly man and woman beside me jumped up and swiftly made their way to the back row, sitting down by other elderly blacks. When I looked back I saw that all of them were trembling as if in fear. I became more puzzled than ever. People walking past began to look at me with keen curiosity. What could it all mean?

When Mama and Liz came back, Mama also had a curious look on her face upon noticing me. "Let's go," she whispered. Once in the car she continued, "You were in the wrong waiting room."

"I saw people in white clothes, and colored clothes, and since I had on colored clothes, I sat down in the colored waiting room," I explained.

WHITE BOY IN THE COLORED SECTION

"No, that means for colored *people*. And the other one is for white people. You should have sat in the white waiting room."

I felt that whirring of numb confusion swelling up again. My mouth felt dry and quivery before I could reply, "Is that why everybody was looking at me funny?"

"Were they? I imagine they were. They'd probably never seen a *white boy in the colored section*."

I had experienced many cultural shocks in Rome, but this one really bowled me over. I sat numb and speechless all the way home. This was a rule made not jointly by whites and blacks, but by the whites who ran the world. But why would venerable old black folk be afraid of a little nine year old white boy, who had actually invaded their own turf?

Then came Lula. During summer break Louise had two weeks' vacation. A substitute maid was recommended and hired. She was a little elderly woman named Lula. She had no uniform. She dressed like the old days with her little maid cap, apron, and long dress. I quickly summed Lula up as a self-possessed little woman who feared no one. She had grown up on a remote farm and was not fearful of racial status on a minute-by-minute basis. In short, she told us what to do, and saw that we did it, post haste. There was no sassing or lollygagging with Lula. Yet before her two weeks were up, we came to see she had a kind streak in her which we would seek to evoke.

Lula would never eat our food. She would make us lunch, then go off and eat her own which she had brought. She usually brought ham biscuits, the biscuits being made from scratch; real country cuisine made by a longtime country gal who now resided in the city housing projects. Though meat biscuits have long been a staple for breakfast at fast-food establishments in America, at that time they were unheard of except among very rural people. And although today I enjoy ham, sausage, or bacon biscuits regularly, I felt a twinge of pity for her being so unsophisticated as to eat a biscuit with a slice of ham stuck inside it. It simply was not in vogue.

TURNER

I am sure we tested the otherwise fiery Lula for her patience, due to her diminutive stature. I would go so far as to say we tested her to the limits. It was not in us kids to sass or taunt her personally, but to see how much noise or scuffling we could get away with despite her increasingly serious admonitions. One day she had Stephen and me go outside and quit rough-housing. We continued our antics on the driveway. We were so unruly she could not hear her favorite television program, so she emerged with a switch to quieten us.

"Come hyar, you boys!" she cried. "I done tolt you to be quiet, and now hyar you carryin' on like wildcats!"

Stephen and I, usually very compliant boys, decided we could avoid a whipping by running. We ran to the edge of the yard, but halted at the street. After all, we hadn't permission to leave the yard.

"I said come hyar!" By now some neighbor kids could see what was happening, and we were too embarrassed to let them see us get a whipping. We stood our ground, though with marked trepidation.

One neighbor boy asked, "Is she trying to give y'all a whoopin'?" We nodded in quiet shame. "Well, she can't do that to y'all! You're white and she's colored!" I started to explain that Lula had permission to discipline us, but words failed me. I felt embarrassment at what we had done to her, and the fix we had gotten ourselves into.

Lula was so mad she threw the switch down. She started to run after us, but due to her age she gave up after only three paces. Then her big dynamo of fortitude, hidden within her little frame, whirred into action as she called out, "I'm gonna call yo' Papa and tell him to brang you some kretches, 'cause I'm *sho'* gonna break yo' *laigs!*"

Partly out of pity for Lula, but mostly for fear of her calling Daddy, we slowly inched our way back toward her. We quietly apologized, after glancing back to make sure the other kids did not see our repentant posturing. She cooled down and we never got the whipping, but she did not talk to us the rest of the day. I thought a long time on her threat to break our legs. I reassured myself that this was only a metaphor for a sound thrashing with the switch, and not an actual potential for her to stomp and twist on our legs, snapping them in two. But I think she could have done it, given enough wind.

So long as we were quiet and behaved, Lula was actually not bad company. Moreover, she reminded me of my grandmothers in her general old-timey manner; especially sharing words of folk wisdom and inspiration for daily life. After watching a program with her on TV, she would always turn her head, peer toward us through her horn rimmed glasses, and share a moral to the story. Following a crime or courtroom drama, she would turn to us and say, "Um-*hmmm*. It just go to show: crime do not pay!"

"Lula, why do you work?" I asked her one day.

"Why, I gots to pay bills, young man!"

"Bills. Bills are mean. When I grow up, I'm never going to pay bills!"

Lula's moral-alert went off. She went right to work admonishing me. "You don't pay yo' bills, you know wha' happen? You turn on de lights; no light. You turn on de stove; no stove. You open de fridge; no food. If you wants to live, you pays yo' bills! Dat's a part of life! You'll see one day. An' dat's why people work."

"Well, I heard people can quit school at sixteen, and go to work. I'm going to, when I turn sixteen. Then I'll be free." (I suddenly gulped on recognizing my use of the word "free." I felt awkward for Lula's sake. But she went on, unaffected by my social *faux pas*.)

"What, you like diggin' ditches, boy? 'Cause dat's what you'll be a-doin' for de rest of yo' life, if you quits school!"

"Why?" I stammered.

"Well, 'cause you won't know nothin'. Or not know enough of nuthin'. Dey only gives good jobs to folks who is smart, and has learnt all dey can."

"About what?"

"Everything! You just gots to get yourself smart in everything you can. My boy thought *he'd* be smart, and quit school. Now he dig ditches; and hopin', just *hopin'*, he can get a better job on de garbage truck!" She shook her head briskly. "Nawsuh, you wants to do better dan dat!"

I resolved then and there to stay in school. I would have anyway. (Nine years of college and three degrees!) I was just talking big, to sound big. But Lula's sage advice shored up the standards of my upbringing, and I was deeply impressed that she was such a wise, viable entity in a world where blacks were supposed to be somehow less than us, socially. Indeed, Lula's overall composition and demeanor reminded me of every elderly white woman I had ever known—same wisdom, same seriousness; same concern for the wellbeing of young children—and I believed every word she uttered from then on.

We grew closer. She would share wonderful stories with us. We would sit spellbound as she told of her life as a girl, picking cotton with her parents and grandmother.

"My grandma was a slave, in de old days. She never had much of nothin' as a girl. And when she got freed, she still had nothin'. She kept on working on her old massa's place, jes' like nothin' had changed. She married one of the field hands on dat farm, and my mama growed up pickin' cotton too. Den 'long came me. I picked it too. Same farm, same cotton. Like nuthin' had changed."

"Were you like a slave?" Stephen asked. I gave him a big-brother glare for his impertinence, but Lula went right on as if it was cool. She was very matter-of-fact.

"Naw, honey. But it weren't much diff'rent, as far as de work. An po'. Mercy, child, we was po'. An' never seen nothin' of de outside world."

We sat all agog. These were the centennial years of the American Civil War, and a lot of hoopla was being made over it; at least, in the white world. Movies and TV programs were full of Civil War dramas, and we boys even had toy Confederate hats and muskets.

Lula went on, "One day I spied an aeroplane so high in de sky, I axed Granny, 'What dat thing a-flyin' so high up yonder?' Granny couldn't hear it, and just gave a glance up and said, 'Why, a big old bird, honey child,' and went on about her work. But I watched it go on, and I allowed it was something magic. Planes was new, an' we'd never heared-tale of 'em."

WHITE BOY IN THE COLORED SECTION

Then came the old folk tales, which were probably so ancient that they came from Africa. The one that has stayed with me most, is the tale of the witch's children. Lula recounted the events:

"Dare were dis woman who was a witch. An' every night when de young'uns was asleep, she'd take off her skin, hang it up, and go a-flyin' off on her broom." We sat rapt and immovable. "Den one night her younguns seen her do it, and allowed dey's gwine fix her from dat evildoin'. So de next night, after she hung up her skin and flew off, de younguns took and poured salt all inside her skin, and hung it back up. Den dey tore off to bed. When she come back just 'fore daylight, she pulled her skin back on, and de salt set to burnin'. She let out a long, loud scream, jumped back on her broom, flew away howlin', and *never* come back! And dat was de end of dat witch! Umm, umm, umm." She swayed her head for emphasis.

We had never heard such tales before. We all sat in silence for some time, marveling over its uniqueness and sheer horror, and pondering—if only for a second—if it could have been true. After all, she told them with as much seriousness as she did everything else. To this day I regret that there was no one around to record her old tales. I have never heard the like of them since. There were many, some which were more uplifting, but this one stuck with me these fifty three years.

I got so that I no longer noticed Lula's being from a different race than us. She was a genuine, individualistic person focused keenly on life, and always knew what to do to solve our problems—with a choice moral always thrown into the scenario. She was such a unique jewel, and had much to contribute to our daily life for those two short weeks—weeks which in retrospect seem like a much longer time. On her last day, Mama was set to drive her to the bus stop, and called out, "Kids, say goodbye to Lula!" We said "Bye" and waved to her as she got into the car. But there was much more going on than that. I had developed feelings for her, and wanted her to know it. To this day I wish I had said, "It has been a wonderful experience, Lula.

You have made a big impression on our young lives. We hope to see you again, Lula!" But we never did.

Missing Lula was assuaged by the return of Louise. She patted us boys on the head and hugged little Laura and Liz. Soon Lula was a memory and we were back to our old routine. I felt sorry for Louise one summer day when we were in the yard, and the garbage truck rolled up. She walked to the street and shared a brief word with one of the men on the truck. He said something very succinct to her, and away they rolled. They hardly acknowledged each other.

I asked, "Louise, do you know that man?" I thought it was neat to finally see two black people interact, and to observe even more evidence that they were people who did things and felt things much like us.

"He's my husband," she replied quietly, almost with embarrassment for having communicated outside the household while on duty. "I just needed to ask him something."

Even at my tender age, I could readily see the sadness of this scenario. Being finite integers within the binding and debasing role of servitude, they hadn't the liberty to even communicate as man and wife; at least not while serving white folks.

Amos n' Andy: A major milestone in my cultural awareness occurred with reruns of the "Amos n' Andy" television program, which began airing. I did not know that the show originated in 1951. Now it was over ten years later when we kids discovered it, and we thought it was brand new. Moreover, it was fascinating to observe black folks in their own world, *"as they really were!"* I was so pleased to see that the cast wore nice suits and dresses, and lived rather as we did, all civilized and with access to the comforts of modern civilization.

The main character, Kingfish, was hilarious in his constant scheming. His wife Sapphire, a decent lady, rather reminded me of Louise, and kept Kingfish in line. Most of the characters seemed intelligent and respectable, with the exception of the third-rate lawyer Calhoun, and addle-brained cab driver Lightning. At the time, I never thought of Calhoun and Lightning as being an embarrassment to black folks. I thought that was just the way some black people were, and I always laughed at them. Some of the boys would imitate Lightning and get a big laugh out of it. In its own warped way, it was opening the door slightly for whites to discuss the touchy subject of blacks.

The words of Mama, "Never make fun of colored people," rang a guilty alarm in the back of my mind. But I reasoned that "Amos n' Andy" was just innocent comedy, and always ended with a good moral once Kingfish acknowledged the error of his ways, and repented. But we kids loved to watch his scheming, and his hilarious attempts at getting gain over others. The laugh track sounded like black accented voices, and occasionally one could hear a jivey voice call out, *"Oh, yeah!"* amongst the dubbed-in laughter. I was sure colored folks were proud to have their own television show. It came as a surprise years later to learn that many blacks considered the show demeaning.

Some whites would comment, "That Kingfish is just like a *n______r*, sneaking around and acting a fool." I didn't believe it, especially since most of the cast were so nicely behaved. But it was a characterization I would hear many times in life, about a great many blacks, real or hypothetical—enough to ponder now and then if there was an element of truth in it.

My walk to school was about half a mile. I would always watch the ditches to and fro for discarded pop bottles to redeem at Haney's Store, about half way twixt home and school. Those found enroute to school were hidden in the end of a culvert, to be redeemed on the homeward trek. Those found going home were redeemed immediately. Three bottles would fetch you six cents in refunded deposits. Five cents was all you needed to by a treat or a bottle of pop; there was no sales tax for purchases under ten cents back then. Stephen and I would share in all such booty. Stopping at Haney's Store also gave us time to browse his little rack of toys, and to observe the comings and goings of various people. Haney's was like a microcosmic hub of civilization. I was particularly impressed with hard-sell salesmen pressuring him to make an order for their wares. The delivery men, bringing in several boxes of candy bars or other treats at a time, set my food fantasies to flight.

Sometimes we would see black domestic workers waiting for the city bus about twenty yards in front of the store. A large cedar tree blocked the view, so Mr. Haney probably seldom saw black people near his establishment. It took me awhile to observe that the black passengers always gravitated toward the back of the bus. I thought on it momentarily now and then, and just figured they liked to sit together. Then one day an odd incident occurred while Stephen and I were in the store: one of the black women at the bus stop approached the store doorway, something I had never seen there before. She stopped in the entrance, kept her eyes low, and asked Mr. Haney, "Suh, it aw-rite if I come in and fetch a loaf of bread?" Mr. Haney nodded silently, and she walked meekly to the bread section. A white customer, a man of average appearance, remarked to Mr. Haney, "Don't they have their own stores? Next thing ya know, they'll be wantin' to take over!"

1962:

Approaching age ten, I was allowed to stay up a little later at night, and discovered an entertaining TV comedy called "The Jack Benny Program." Jack had a black *valet—major domo—factotum* called Rochester. Rochester stood his own ground and counseled Jack, and helped keep him on an even keel with life. Though clearly in a servant's role, he was also Jack's friend and was treated almost like an equal. I probably spent as much time analyzing this as I did trying to understand the comedic situations. After all, our schools and my entire world were still segregated, and with the exception of Louise, I had no contact with blacks. I had no real idea of what the black world was like, or how blacks factored into society. But here was a white man, the big star Jack Benny, freely conversing with a black man. Boys on the school playground would imitate Rochester's gravelly voice and always receive laughter in response. It became popular for a brief time to try to impersonate Rochester. The main thing was that people seemed to like and respect him enough to receive him into their homes via television screen on a weekly basis.

The old "Our Gang" films began to air on local television. There were black boys in the series, named Buckwheat and Stymie. They were full-fledged members of their coterie of pals, and though they were not leaders, they were equals. The amazing thing about this was that they were filmed mainly in the 1920's and 1930's, at a very high point of segregation. I didn't know what to make of it, but was more interested in the comedy situations than in figuring out how the black boys got cast in the films. I do remember remarking once to my parents, "Look, they've got colored boys in this movie." It was no big deal to them, but a marvel to me.

Soon after this time, an occasional black performer would be seen on a predominantly white variety show, usually singers such as Lena Horne or Nat King Cole. But even these roles were rare, and restricted to singers who had such high record sales that they could not be ignored by producers, and who would be reasonably accepted by white audiences. I recall how much my parents and grandparents loved to watch singers on TV. After a particularly good performance by any black artist on a variety show, my Grandpa Turner would remark, "I reckon colored people were put on this earth to entertain!" Since these were the only blacks his community ever saw within the all-white Appalachian region of Georgia, his opinion seemed logical.

I never watched the TV news as a kid. But when I would walk through the den, I would take a glance at the screen in passing. There seemed to be increasing numbers of blacks on the evening news, assembled for one cause or another I did not understand. I do remember one marching group wearing signs and hats that read "We Want Jobs." I stopped and asked Daddy why they are saying they want jobs. He didn't respond; he just kept watching. After all, it was a subject of embarrassment.

When we came to Rome, Daddy was a special county agent for the University of Georgia Cooperative Extension Service. In addition to educating the county's farmers on technique and appearing on a weekly radio broadcast and occasional television program, he was also in charge of 4-H. Brother Martin was a star 4-H'er. Daddy was his mentor at 4-H meetings and projects, and accompanied him and his local club to 4-H camp. It never occurred to me that blacks were being excluded from these programs, despite it being funded from taxes, until years later when I was in 4-H. Daddy was not in favor of discrimination or denial of participation; he was caught up in the age-old system: colors don't mix. Blacks had to pay the same taxes, but did not get the same benefits.

But at this time Daddy resumed his education and became a vocational rehabilitation counselor. As a matter of course, he did serve a number of handicapped black clientele. But until this time, his government service had excluded contact with black citizens—fellow taxpayers. His new professional role and positive interaction with blacks happened years before our schools were integrated, and though I am confident he strove to provide them the very finest rehabilitative services, I do not recall him ever discussing black clients' cases. They simply were not a subject for discussion.

PART 2:   THE ROTTEN EGG GETS CRACKED

1963:

In August, Dr. Martin Luther King made his historic "I Have A Dream" speech at the Lincoln Memorial in Washington, DC. I never even heard about it until I was grown. I am certain it was covered by the press, and in viewing videos and photographs of the event, it appears most of the audience were white. It has made a historical and enduring impact; yet I was totally unaware of it. Life simply carried on, born upon gentle Southern winds that were about to transform into tempests. But I could not see it at the time.

We moved from West Rome out to a nice suburban neighborhood called Sequoia Acres. We were on the edge of the country and the Rome city busses did not come out our way. This meant that one of my parents would have to drive into town to pick up Louise. Mama usually did it. On the first day that Daddy picked her up, some of the rowdier boys on my school bus started jeering at me as they saw Louise emerge from the car with him.

"You've got a colored Mama?" one of them jeered. Then turning to some others, he continued, "Hey, Turner here has a *n______r* mama!"

"No I don't!" came my immediate reply.

"Oh yeah you do. I seen her gittin' outta the car with your daddy!"

"He's just bringing her to work!"

"Then you're a *n______r* lover!" Hey y'all, Turner's a *n______r* lover!"

"No I am not!" My respect for Louise and my civil upbringing notwithstanding, I recoiled at this intended insult. My primal childish response was to reject ridicule, not blacks *per se*. They could have called me anything, and I would have made the same comeback. Ridicule hurts in any form. But the seeds of prejudice and segregation were being planted within me by the power of social pressure, whether I realized it or not, as I subconsciously began to inculcate a vein of cultural bias.

Even the polite kids, too nice to verbally assault anyone, looked skeptically at me with a budding spark of fear and rejection ready to spring from their eyes. They, too, would have surely rejected me if I had demonstrated the slightest inclination toward favoring blacks, though their "good manners" would not allow them to confront me directly. It was the collective unconscious—the ever-flowing tide of racial bias which made city bus drivers glare at a black passenger if he did not move fast enough to the rear seats. It was the common mental denominator which automatically told blacks to keep walking when approaching a white business establishment or public entertainment event. Never in my life did I witness racial violence or public protest, Ku Klux Klan activities, etc. Perhaps far stronger was this ever-present social orientation that cemented racism in place and caused it to survive so long.

The new school I attended was, for the most part, rather oafish. There were a number of refined suburbanite kids there, but the roughnecks were overwhelming. I was in sixth grade and had never been in a real fight before. Yet here I found myself in serious fisticuffs practically every day, mostly being tried out as the new boy from the city school system. I soon garnered the nickname City Slicker. And although I was by no means spoiled, some boys resented my nice, clean clothes. The boys whose pants had patches sewn onto them seemed to give me the hardest time. I would soon learn that they were also the type who most disdained people of color.

This school had gotten the bright idea of separating boys' and girls' classes from sixth through eighth grades. Add to this the fact that there were several big toughs in sixth who should have been in eighth or ninth, and you had a rowdy bunch on your hands. Ironically, although this rural area had far fewer blacks than the city did, for some reason I was beginning for the first time to hear a lot of students making disparaging remarks about blacks in general.

WHITE BOY IN THE COLORED SECTION

If a boy wore a new item of clothing, someone would invariably ask, "How far did you have to chase that n______r before you stole that off of him?" If there were a fight between two boys, call them Johnny and Billy—and if Billy were the least liked overall—a crowd would begin to gather around them and chant, "Fight! Fight! A black and a white! Billy's the black, and Johnny's the white!" If a sloppy looking car drove by the school, some boy might say, "There goes a real n______ered-up hunk of junk!"

The Civil Rights Movement was getting its first real gust of wind in its sails, and resultantly blacks were being shown and mentioned at a slightly but steadily increasing rate via all media forms. A proportionate increase in racial slurs began to be manifest, and I heard boys often remark about how they hated blacks, and that they ought to go back to slavery!

When word got around the class that a black woman had been seen at my house, I was confronted by nearly half the class one day while the teacher was out of the room. One large, ill-mannered boy kept bumping me around with his oversized belly, and saying, "Hey, Turner, we hear you've got a n______r mama!" Several voices joined in with, "Yeah! We don't allow no colored boys around here!"

"I do not!" was the only response I could produce. I was both terrified and humiliated.

"Well, what about that n______r gal who is always being seen at your house?"

"She's our maid! She works for us!"

One boy in the crowd, just as racist as the rest but with a more benign temperament, twistedly interceded on my behalf with the remark, "Why, his family is just keeping that colored gal where she belongs! Sort of like a slave, right, Turner?"

I stammered for a few moments while several potential responses milled about in my mind. I wanted to tell them that my parents taught me to be nice to colored folks, that Louise was a good woman who worked hard for us, that we only wanted to give her employment and not degradation, etc. But I knew these would probably only result in more hazing and possibly a mob beating. So under the horrendous pressure of the moment, I meekly blurted, "Yeah."

I felt guilty for my desperate reply, but adding to the guilt was my sense of relief as the boys began to pat me on the back and turn away. One of them said, "Yeah, they ain't good fer nuthin' but pickin' cotton!" Another responded with, "Yeah, and the really smart'uns get to be janitors and garbage men!" It suddenly dawned on me that there were no black janitors in the schools I had attended, nor any black employees in any position, not even the lunch room. Even the menial jobs were segregated. I doubt a black employee would have long endured the seething racial environment at this school anyway.

In those days a principal or employer or personnel manager could be heard to say with total impunity, "We don't want any coloreds working for us," or "We gotta watch out not to let any coloreds amongst our children," etc. It didn't even have to be mentioned; it was a given, and commonly understood.

So moving a very few miles across town brought me to another end of the racial spectrum. Instead of it being merely impolite to discuss race where racism was subtle, now suddenly I was flung headlong into an environment where it was discussed openly, albeit only in a derogatory, hurtful way. Still, it was not a topic students mentioned in front of faculty, nor vice versa; at least, not for now.

Everyone who was alive on November 22, 1963 remembers where he or she was, and what they were doing, when President Kennedy was shot. I was sitting in sixth grade boys' study hall, last period of the day. Due to space deficits, we were assigned seats in the same room where high schoolers were taking typing class. It was like trying to read while a covey of woodpeckers hammered away. Looking out the window I saw the typing teacher running from the other building toward ours, with a startled look on his face. He interrupted the class to announce that President Kennedy had been shot in Dallas, Texas, and taken to a hospital. Absolute quiet fell over the room, and no one spoke.

As we sat in our homeroom waiting to be dismissed for the day, one of the older boys called out to everyone, *"Y'all, the president is dead!"*

"How do you know?" some boys asked.

"Because they just lowered the school flag to half mast!"

The bus ride home was eerily silent. When I entered the house, I called out, "Louise, did you hear about..."

Louise was ironing and watching the TV, and earnestly sobbing. My words failed me, on their own. I just stood and watched her with pity. She kept wagging her head, weeping, and ironing. Finally she moaned, "He was just trying to help the colored people!" I didn't know that he had done anything for them, but I was forever touched by the image of this black woman mourning the passing of a white man.

Then within one shocking, revelatory moment it became pointedly insightful to see that colored people were not inexorably devoted to the *status quo* of racial order; not inherently content to stay "in their place." I had heard some whites speak of "good coloreds knowing their place," and "being a credit to their race." Apparently both phrases meant the exact same thing.

All the blacks I had seen heretofore always seemed to bear up with dignity while mingling amongst their own people. Although traditionally tending to cower when around white folks, and even at this time in modern history likely to feel withdrawn and aloof, they seemed to function as freely and happily as did we within their own social element—on their own turf. I could see it when we drove past black neighborhoods or gatherings, and was always enthralled to see them socialize with their heads up, signifying that they were, indeed, people like us and capable of advancing from their lowered state.

And now here was Louise opening my eyes to that reality with one simple, tear-laden statement, "He was just trying to help the colored people." My thoughts of Kennedy and the sad plight of our nation faded as my heart swelled with pity and compassion for Louise. I sat on the sofa and watched the TV coverage with Stephen. Laura was just old enough to understand what had happened, minus the comprehension of its social and national impact. But toddler Lizzie was too young to really grasp the significance of what had happened. Martin was away at boarding school, so it was basically Stephen and I watching entranced, as Laura plied away with numerous questions: "Who? Why? How?" All we could do was observe the entire world change before us, in unbelief, as Louise sobbed and wagged her head.

I went upstairs and sat on my bed, laying out my books. I lay down and pondered toward the ceiling what Louise had said. It was almost as novel and astonishing as the assassination. Louise mourned the loss not of a "beloved white master" but of potential advancement for her people. She was my only contact with the black world, yet surely she represented all of them. She grieved for all of them. So, black people wanted more. They wanted to be truly free, a century after the slaves were legally liberated. What did this mean for the future? What was their hope?

Did Kennedy's death set them back? If they did advance, what would happen to the white-dominated world?

I had recently joined a Boy Scout troop comprised of boys from my school. We went on a five mile hike one cool day. We were surprised by a half foot of snow that fell on us. The scoutmaster led us to shelter at an old place he called the Higgenbotham Plantation. We went inside the abandoned manor house and explored its two floors and several rooms. It was in a shambles, and people had knocked out many of the windows. The scoutmaster, detecting a couple of our boys doing the same, had us leave the house and take shelter in a long, low cabin made of square-cut logs.

We gathered some wood and built a fire in the fireplace. Not until I had my feet warming up to the fire did someone point out that this old structure had been a slave cabin! I lay there marveling at the fading yet not-quite-dead history of it all, antiquity crossing paths with the modern age, and the stark contrast of the big house and the little house. One had once ruled ominously over the other. Now it didn't matter much anymore: the big house was rendered totally unattractive by the ravages of time facilitated by abandonment. The Spartan cabins, rustic as they perhaps always had been, still stood strong. The structures that separated master from slave were now simultaneously returning to Mother Earth, and the souls who lived there in their respective roles had gone on to equality in the next world. God grant that we can learn this lesson while still in this world; perhaps we will work together to make it a better world while there are still generations being born into it. The house and cabin represented for me the state of affairs in which I currently lived. The past, long gone, was still looming in our cultural consciousness, yet surely fading into obscurity as the new world was rapidly approaching ahead.

More black entertainers were beginning to be seen on televised variety shows, and at the same time more black issues were coming to the surface on the news broadcasts, though mostly negative or disturbing events. I do not know if our parents' enforcing our homework hours intentionally coincided with the evening TV news, but I seldom watched it and remained generally oblivious concerning black issues. Then one day a boy approached me before class and exclaimed, "Did you hear the good news? Eight black Muslims were shot and killed in New York!" He grinned with what one would readily detect as gleeful satisfaction.

"What's that? Who are they?" I asked.

"Why, black Muslims are n______rs that want to take over the country! They were fighting with police, and a bunch got shot! Boy, that's great!"

"What do you mean, take over?" A jolt of fear shot through me. This was an alien subject to me, and sounded ominous.

"Yeah, that'll learn them n______rs ," another boy chimed in.

Stunned as usual upon witnessing such brusqueness, I was relieved to see the teacher enter the room as all voices fell silent. Even in this school, the subject of race was still taboo, as far as the adults were concerned. There would be no more talk about this unusual shocking occurrence until I got home, and at the dinner table asked, "Mama, Daddy. What's a black Muslim?"

The air stood still. Voices remained quiet. Daddy softly mumbled something about not talking about it at the table. Mama added that we could talk about it later, reinforcing that it was not a polite topic over dinner. I was too embarrassed to bring it up again. I never did get an answer to my question, and soon the topic faded.

By Fall I was in the seventh grade. There was a particularly delinquent boy in sixth who was always perpetrating serious mischief. He looked dishonest from the start, and seldom did a day go by without his being sent to the principal's office. He stole, he committed vandalism, and incited students into fighting over empty accusations he claimed one had made against another. His beady eyes always seemed to reflect a mind fixated on some antisocial rascality or another. He came from an ignorant and impoverished social background; not that poverty is automatically a sign of low virtue. But with it came an obvious lack of refinement and social values. There were no visible components within his personality makeup that could foster any visible merit on his part.

One day he was riding his bicycle to school and wrecked it on a dirt road. He was late to school. His clothes were torn and muddy, and his knees and arms skinned and lightly bleeding.

The principal intercepted him as he came sneaking up to the school entrance. Rather than merely explaining why he was late, he had to provide a story to cover his embarrassment. His little tale soon exploded into a major scare for the entire community.

He claimed that while he was enroute to school, two colored guys jumped him and knifed him! The school was on alert, and some faculty were assigned to make a security patrol of the campus. Soon we could see through my classroom windows the fields and woods being scoured by very serious-looking county police officers and sheriff's deputies. Shotguns, dogs, the shouting of commands back and forth: an entire 19th Century scene played out before our eyes.

Recess was cancelled, and we had to be escorted by a detail of faculty to the lunch room. After lunch as I sat in my next class, the teacher, a young and aggressive man, remarked, "If I catch me one of those c____ns, I'm gonna take him by the ears and rub his face up and down a pine tree!" Right there, in front of the class, in public school and on government time, he made this racial threat against nonexistent criminals, reaping the reply of "Yeah! That's right!" from many of the boys in the room.

When the teacher stepped out in the hall to speak with another faculty member for a moment, one boy voiced a twisted version of the command at Bunker Hill, "Don't fire 'til you see the blacks of their faces!" The statement began to be echoed around the room until the teacher reentered, whereupon the banter fell silent.

Some of the polite boys, myself included, said nothing. Some kept their eyes focused downward away from the teacher. He was one who liked to single boys out as being less manly if they did not seem to agree with some of his macho talk. I resented his brash manner at first. To date I had never heard a white make such a violent remark against blacks, especially within the semi-sanctity of the classroom.

But believing, as did everyone else, that the incident actually did occur, I deep inside felt the teacher's anger—and the slightest twinge of admiration for what my juvenile and gullible mind perceived as a sort of heroism on his part. My feelings toward blacks were beginning to sort themselves between shining benevolence, to benign apathy, and on down to moderate resentfulness, and I was being caught up within an emotional conflict because of it.

Occasionally through the day I would overhear teachers in the hallways mentioning the latest news on the "assault" situation, in whispered tones, looking about to discern whether any of the school kids were listening. It was being mentioned that the black community was all scared and remaining in hiding, for fear of reprisals. There was talk of whites carrying guns and keeping armed watch over their property. It was just like the slave days or years of Postbellum strife in that respect. Many feared that there would be a local riot or civil disturbance.

"My daddy's ready for them *n______rs*," I heard more than one boy say. "Got his shotgun loaded and standing by the door!" There was a militant feeling in the air. Perhaps it was a prideful rebound from the failure of the old Confederacy. Or was it just the nature of things, to hate those of other races? Regardless, I could sense deeply that it was real life, happening in real time.

The scenario being rumored to be a hoax was never announced officially. Apparently too much pride and embarrassment were involved. The word was spread mouth to ear by students that the boy had fabricated the entire story, and caused the resultant panic. No mention was ever made concerning any punishment, if any, he had received. The incident was entirely hushed up. Was that a condition for his not being subjected to serious punishment or criminal charges, for him to just forget the entire thing and never speak of it? Whatever the case, there was never again any mention of the situation. Apparently the young miscreant's disruptive and criminal act was not as serious to the white authorities. Maybe the colored folk were just not deemed worthy by them of any official respect. He was never charged with anything by the law. Soon the miscreant was back to his usual habits of stealing from the school store, or breaking into vending machines.

I have never been able to erase that day's incidents from my memory. Moreover, it was a day I felt both sorrow for, and disdain toward, the black situation. The disdain began to bud because there came to be almost no end to many whites' complaints about every aspect of black life, and it just seemed like there must have been many generations of white experience to back it up. I became distraught over my mixed feelings. I was so young and unlearned in these matters. I had never known more than a scant trace about the black world, and now I was having to deal with intensive strife over it on a daily basis. Which way was I to turn?

There was a high school on the same campus. Many of the older boys, though no obvious girls, openly voiced their disdain for blacks. Increasingly one heard the comment, "If we don't keep the coloreds under control, they're gonna take over!" If a young boy hears this on a frequent basis, he does begin to ponder the likelihood from time to time. He will also very likely begin to develop some degree of wariness of their potential and motive to do so. Although most whites were mute on the subject, those with audible voices were very biased racially, and their loud grumbling was difficult to altogether ignore.

The stress was in the air, thick as smoke. "If things are this bad when most whites have never even spoken to a black," I mused, "how is it going to be if the government really tries to integrate us?"

1964:

Shock can rip like lightening through the brightest day. In seventh grade study hall on a nice mild morning, with the windows open and a soothing breeze caressing the face and head, one was almost lulled to sleep as boys quietly read their lessons. But gradually a sideshow began to distract us. We could overhear the elderly man teaching high school civics next to us. He was probably born in the 1890's and was a product of "the old ways." He had subbed in some of my sixth and seventh grade classes, and we held him up as a forthright man of wisdom and propriety, albeit a bit eccentric. He knew endless facts about countless subjects. He was a scholarly and authoritative man one would be hesitant to question or contradict. He often wrought the outward workings of a crusty old curmudgeon, but as long as you stayed on his good side, he was somewhat benign.

But today we overheard him in an entirely different vein of expression and subject matter. He was spouting off to his civics class the supposed virtues of segregation. He was of that order of whites who clung fiercely to the past, truly fearing the apparently impending days of integration.

His every word seemed to almost catch fire in his mouth, spewing flames of anger and disgust not just at black people, but the inevitability that one day our races would be mingled and our sense of social identity would be lost. Studying became difficult as he began to rant, but we were aghast when he proclaimed, "All these colored men want to do is marry a bunch of white women, create a race of orange people, and take over the world!"

We boys began to glance around at each other briefly, eyes reflecting inner fright and confusion. My mind started spinning like a merry-go-round. A kaleidoscope of memories competed for the forefront of my conscious mind: my early childhood where I was unaware of racial differences, my sparse introduction into a world where black people dwelled, adults teaching me to be polite to coloreds but not to talk about them, school teachers never mentioning race at all—and now a government employee, drawing his salary from the taxpayers of all races while taking government time to ragingly sermonize against our "semi-fellow citizens" known as negroes.

And were his claims true? After all, he was a teacher, and he had lived a long time. We students were so shocked with disbelief, that we did not mention his tirade after study hall was over. It was as though all of the boys had been set adrift upon separate seas of their own contemplation over this drastic and frightening proclamation. Was it true, then, that blacks were plotting to take over the nation and society? How could they, when they had scarcely any resources or opportunities at hand? And really create a new race of orange people? He was a teacher; he knew things; I had to ponder this. It was all just too bizarre, but coming from a source of supposed authority it seemed to warrant some pondering and even a bit of fear.

On the bus ride home, my concern was balanced somewhat by recollecting that the teacher was also a bit peculiar and very old fashioned. At dinner I brought the subject up, rather abruptly: "I heard Mr. _______ say that colored men just want to marry a lot of white women, create a race of orange people, and take over the world. Is that true?"

A moment of dead silence fell over the dining room, which, owing to the acute tension I had just created, seemed more like a very long and poignant ordeal. If silence could thunder, it was apt to right then! This sort of comment simply wasn't made, especially at our house. The runaway train was quickly derailed when Daddy managed to choke out the sound of "Hmmph!" followed by a very stern "Don't talk about things like that!"

Stephen looked shocked and keenly curious. "Is that true? Can they do that?" he dared to query.

With a wag of the head, Daddy projected another embarrassed "Hmmph!" The subjected was now cancelled and void; nary another word was uttered over dinner. On the surface it could appear that Daddy was confirming my inquiry by instructing me to not mention it, but I could readily discern from his demeanor and emotions that the teacher's claim was extremist nonsense. I sensed Daddy knew that. It's just that certain topics were embarrassing and thus unsuitable for discussion between children and adults in those days. After all, this was a generation in which communication over sensitive subjects was taboo.

Within this rather limited communications framework, I went to bed with my concerns at least somewhat assuaged. But the fact that adults were panicked over the state and progress of racial issues could not be denied. It began to progressively surface at school, as more boys began to voice their parents' remarks about blacks and the socio-political situation.

Now Dr. Martin Luther King, Jr. began to be covered often on the TV news as well as in newspapers. I had no idea what was going on, only that he was stirring people up. Sometimes I would leave my bedroom desk where my homework was in progress, and creep halfway down the stairs where I would sit and try to overhear some of the news about Dr. King. Seems he was always being arrested, was all I could gather. On one occasion I tiptoed through the den to get a glass of water in the kitchen, and on the way back, presented the question, "Why is Martin Luther King in trouble again? What's he doing?"

My parents sat in silent embarrassment. I knew they had humane feelings toward blacks, but were also fenced in by the racial standards of the day. They simply did not know what to tell me. I saw the newspaper on the sofa with King on the front page, throwing a punch, while the headlines read "Martin Luther King arrested for assault." It was many years before I would learn that it was actually he who was being assaulted, and in attempting to fend off his attacker, an opportunistic photographer captured him in an unfairly incriminating perspective right before he was unjustly arrested.

Though initially shrouded in social avoidance, the name "Martin Luther King" was gradually becoming a household—and school ground—word, as if it were one word unto itself. He was being held up as an object of ridicule. None of his sayings or teachings were being quoted within my dimension of life. All I ever heard were general remarks of derision by juveniles who had no idea of who he was or what he stood for. He was being caricatured as a trouble maker and "uppity negro." Moreover, I may have been the only youth in my school who had been allowed a peek through the window of the black social wall, for via Louise I had glimpsed a side to their life unbeknownst to the average non-black person. How I wondered what King was really up to. How I pondered over any relevance he may have had to Louise's lamentation and desire to overcome. But the answers were not forthcoming. The only time his name came up, whites would say, "He ought to behave himself. He's stirring up the coloreds so they don't want to behave!"

Everywhere we went, black folks seemed to avoid eye contact or social interaction with whites. They were seen less in public, and stayed indoors as much as possible. Here on the brink of true liberty, they were again ensnared within the fearsome walls of 19th Century persecution. How long could society ignore the volcano on which they all sat? Something had to break. But for now, colored people were still struggling under the leering face of oppression.

My parents bought a new sofa, and offered the old one to Louise. She was pleased to have it; it really was fairly nice, for a used one. Mama got Stephen and me to load it in the station wagon, and off we drove. I knew the route toward town along Kingston Highway, thence right onto Turner McCall Boulevard, and so on. But when we made a right turn into the housing projects, I was captivated by the dark mystique of it all. The few street lights illuminated the old brick apartments rising gradually from the curbside, and on up a gentle hill. There were trees and shrubs, but little grass. Black kids played here and there under the street lights. There was less than a handful of cars parked along the curb, and those were jalopies. It was a different world than I had ever seen, and it both startled and intrigued me.

Soon as we drove up and opened the back of the station wagon, a small crowd formed around the car. "Who y'all here for? Y'all here for somebody?" inquisitive yet respectful young voices chimed. I was surprised that several black youth had the courage to address us white strangers, even on their own exclusive turf. We presented quite a novelty to these kids; you could see the surprise and curiosity on their young faces, as if we were the circus just arriving in town.

Mama replied, "The ______________ family. Could one of you tell Louise we are here?"

A few kids scurried up the hill, and soon Louise and her boys came down to meet us. She instructed her boys to tote the sofa up to their apartment. Stephen and I went too, mainly to see where—and how—they lived. Trudging up some bare, dirty slopes and then some steps, we managed to get the sofa to their apartment. Their father came out and helped the boys, briefly nodding his gratitude. "Thanks, boys. We'll get it from here." He looked shocked to see us, and glanced around as if to discern whether any neighbors were alarmed to see white boys on his porch. They were. Several of them. I didn't know if we were not considered desirable company to come into their abode, or if they were simply embarrassed at the unprecedented event of having whites enter therein. I rather suspected the latter, on peering briefly inside.

They had a kitchen and table. Check. Some cupboards. Check. Old stove and small antique refrigerator. Check. Not much else could I see, that resembled how we lived. A dark hallway seemed to lead into a small living room which was sparse and tight. There was one worn out chair visible. The general condition of the unit was old and depressing, and painted a shabby dull light yellow. From what I could see, all the units appeared to be adorned in the same shabby toneless color. I saw no toys, bicycles, or anything at all attractive about the little neighborhood of subsidized housing. And there were no whites living there. Was that a rule? Or a choice of segregation? Where did poor whites live? I found out later that there were some whites-only housing projects down on Shorter Avenue. There was landscaping there, and more cars and some bikes.

Louise and Mama took to conversing, and within minutes Stephen and I were bored enough to meander off and see how the colored boys would react to us. They were so poor but very polite. After staring at each other with mutual curiosity for a few moments, one of the boys took the words out of my mouth when he asked, "Y'all wanna play?"

"Yeah. What ya playing?" I replied, relieved to feel accepted. In a culture where whites generally felt blacks were honored to have whites condescend to socialize with them, I felt a renewal of human equality in sensing that it was I who wanted to be accepted by them.

"Rasslin'," answered the boy. "You and Steamboat can rassle. Then T-Bone will rassle the winner." He looked at Stephen and said, "You can rassle Turtle. He about your size."

We commenced to wrestling right down there in pure loose soil, in our good school clothes. We practically whipped up a whirlwind of dust, and soon I was brown from head to toe. These were surprisingly strong boys, quick and very adept at athleticism. All the boys were cheering. Girls played house or dolls or skipped rope. Occasionally a boy would look over to see if the girls were watching him be so macho down there in the arena. An image flashed in my mind about how the white boys back at school would do that during football, to see if the cheerleaders were looking at them. Or while fighting, glance over to see if any girls admired them. They never did; they turned up their noses and ignored them. Or pretended to. The black girls reacted the same way. In this regard, these kids were psychologically quite akin to us, and I began to relate to them on a closer social level.

Mama called for us. We slipped furtively into the car without her seeing how dirty we were. On the way home, Stephen said, "Those colored boys have some funny names. Like Steamboat and T-Bone."

"Just nicknames, of course," Mama reassured, smiling softly in the dark.

"They sure are funny!" I added. "And fun to play with, too!"

Mama's tone turned instantly serious. "Don't you boys tell *anybody* at school that you were playing with them tonight! Nobody at all!"

"Why not?"

"Because there could be a mob of furious people in our yard by evening, raising a ruckus and maybe wanting to burn our house down!"

"What people?" I was shocked into near numbness. She might as well have told me the Russians had landed and were conquering our town.

"White people, of course. There are a lot of angry whites right now who are doing all they can to keep us and the colored people apart. So just don't talk about it!"

Stephen lit up and asked, "You mean, we're the first white boys to ever go over and play with those colored boys?"

Mama paid attention to traffic as she made a turn, and then eventually answered, "Probably are. I can only imagine you are. Whites don't even go in there. Maybe they'll drive through for a shortcut from North Broad to

Turner-McCall. But it's their own world. Yes, I imagine you are."

I could not help feeling a rush of pride on receiving that knowledge. I was the first to do something! Someone else was the first to climb Mount Everest, or fly across the ocean. But my brother and I were the first white boys to go into that colored neighborhood and play with the boys who lived there. My fear over Mama's warning was allayed significantly by the pride of knowing I was an intrepid explorer of sorts. Yet I could not even tell anyone!

1965:

I spent much of the summer at the Rome City Pool. White kids swam and sunbathed and listened to Top 40 hits on their transistor radios. Though the subject was never mentioned, it was obvious that blacks were not allowed in the pool, despite their paying taxes to support it. But none of that crossed my mind. It was just a place where white kids went for summer fun. Black kids ran through garden hoses, or went dipping in one of the three rivers in town.

I turned thirteen shortly after the eighth grade began. After a long and bitterly fought battle between school parents and the school board, our high school was taken away and consolidated with two others miles away. Now the only big fight left was the white struggle against integration of the schools. The middle and upper classes did not speak on the subject in public; perhaps in the country club or private parties when ladies were not present, would white gentlemen discuss the seriousness of impending integration.

The working class, however, raged openly against the trend toward desegregation, and their kids would bring their ideas and verbal complaints to school where they were now being heard on a regular basis.

Perhaps the greatest irony was the fact that my mother was the PTA president at our school for two years, yet she never mentioned the bitter strife going on about proposals to consolidate our high school with others, or ultimately perhaps racial integration. There were shouts and threats at some meetings, often directed at school officials but also at anyone who wanted to break apart our little corner of the world with consolidation or integration.

The outlook for our local school, let alone society in general, seemed bleak. For my family at least, what happened in the meetings stayed in the meetings. It simply was not decent conversation for the home. Besides, it was embarrassing and socially dangerous to talk about people in any negative way, especially people who had yelled and threatened in a public meeting. What if it would get around that we had gossiped about them! What, indeed. Except for a couple of boys at school who were not afraid to quote their parents' remarks about the battlefield of the PTA meetings, I would never have known how serious the situation was.

There was such a sharp contrast between overheard words of whites, and of blacks, in public places while witnessing the same events. If a radio were playing somewhere and an announcement were made about some great achievement made by a black, one or two whites within hearing range would often grumble about them getting "uppity." Any blacks standing about would cheer briefly but intensely. As if feeling a moment's relief from centuries of oppression they would shake with jubilation, and then just as quickly mask their feelings. Broadcast statements such as "________ was voted most valuable player in his league," "Negro scientist ________ just discovered a new miracle drug," " Mr. ________ was the first negro elected to public office in the state of ________," would be followed by "Oh! Thank you Lord!" Tears would be shed and abiding smiles would stretch across faces, but their audible glee would soon cease so as not to make a public spectacle.

The same would occur if a black noticed a newspaper headline favorable to blacks, such as "Dr. ________, negro professor, recognized as top scholar at University of ________, " or "Negro college receives presidential award."

I have seen this occur in public places, mainly supermarkets, always with the result of feeling briefly frozen in time as the novelty sank in. My emotions were a combination of amazement and sympathy. On one hand I was glad to see the colored folks get an ego boost. But deep inside, my own culture would seep upward a miniscule amount of eruptive magma, comprised of a fear of losing social superiority. Then guilt would creep in and extinguish the potentially budding beast of bigotry, and I would walk away marveling over these little sunbeams brightening black people's lives for the space of a blink, how much this meant to their poor souls, and especially how little by little society was crawling onward toward another ultimate state. Would it result in happiness? Tumult? This sentiment seemed to pervade the collective white mind.

With increased media coverage of black achievements, the more outspoken white racists would proportionately mouth quite opposite views. I heard one boy exclaim, "Can you believe Nat King Cole's funeral cost $10,000?" (This was a very tidy sum in 1965, when the average funeral cost closer to $700; a fairly nice house could be bought for $10,000. Moreover, the average annual salary then was $4700.)

A friend of his added, "How about that, a *n*________ with that kind of money, showing off like that! Something ain't right." Heads would wag and disgust would be displayed across their countenances. It seemed as though it were a sin or social aberration for blacks to achieve or earn a good living. Secretly, however, I was at least a little stunned to think there were wealthy black people in the world, and I couldn't help fretting a bit over that. I wanted to be glad for them, but that undercurrent of bigotry would endeavor to surface. I did not want to get swept away by its mighty flow, but I have to admit there was a twinge of— shall we label it—*resentment?* I could not fathom even a trace of goodwill for a wealthy black, yet I pitied their poor. It was the perpetual paradox of prejudice. Was I a carrier? This troubled me deep inside.

I soon observed that no one but poor white boys made such hostile remarks against blacks. But it was not simply the jealousy from their being poor; there were many kind and virtuous poor kids around who would never have made such remarks. But it was beginning to look like a combination of poverty and low self-esteem might be contributing factors to such bigoted statements. The well-to-do boys seldom made racist remarks, considering such verbiage beneath them; yet within their hearts they generally wanted segregation as a matter of cultural nature. Rarely but clearly would come a comment from preppier boys to the extent of, "Now, look at that dilapidated car, patched back together. A prime example of Afro-engineering."

The general white consensus, as far as I was exposed to it, was that our kind did not want their kind to win. It was perhaps akin to the animosity one ball team feels toward another; we can't let the other guys win, because that means we add up to less than what we want to be. Sure, that must be it. But from whence did these foul waters spring? Was it the age-old beastly tendency of humankind? The beast that ministers proclaimed we need to restrain and eliminate from ourselves? The Mr. Hyde that Dr. Jekyll could not suppress? Or just the troublesome devilish spirit that has kept the world in turmoil through the ages?

To this very day I am surprised at the trace of racism that exists to some extent within all peoples, and probably most individuals, whether they are aware of it or not. Regardless, I could at least vaguely perceive that despite my benevolent views toward blacks, I secretly did not want them to "take over," if it would truly mean losing my culture and heritage. It was onerous for a boy to shoulder. I didn't cause the problem, so why should I suffer for it? Since the Civil War, most whites claimed the freed blacks could not advance; and at best, they should maintain a "separate but equal" existence. But now a century later, it was not working out that way. I was glad to hear of blacks achieving some pride, but could not express that in front of whites. At the same time, I was scared they might achieve too much, proving we were not as mighty as we had assumed. And if they merely merged with us but did not "take over," I still wondered where that would lead us. Who were we? Where were we headed?

TURNER

As the school integration issue continued to gain steam, racist anger voiced by the unruliest students increased proportionately. In public places, angry white men would complain loudly among themselves about how "the *n______rs* are getting everything they want! The government's gonna let 'em take over, before ya know it!"

What were they getting? What was the government giving to them that would erode the white man's world? How was a barely thirteen year old boy to understand the concerns of these troubled white adults? Contemporary social issues were not taught or discussed in school. Every concept taught in social studies reflected the notion that older days than ours were the standard for life today.

I began to tiptoe into the den at home and listen in more, during the TV news. There was often a segment about negroes, as they called them, wanting something or another. There were scenes of relatively small protests and even fewer marches, often with white police officers surrounding them. Over the weeks, some arrests were shown being made. I didn't get it. In those days kids did not interrupt adults during TV viewing; it could not be paused or rewound. So I had little insight into what the colored folk were wanting. I was sure it was something about rights, but blacks "weren't supposed" to get angry or unruly in public, and thus their voices were not loud at this juncture. The "good negro" image still prevailed, but was apparently being eroded—unpeeling a layer at a time. And inasmuch as I hadn't the slightest interaction with the black world beyond brief words of courtesy with Louise, it was impossible to conjecture why the ones on TV were unhappy. I didn't quite catch what the TV announcers were saying the blacks wanted.

One evening I waited for a commercial interruption, and quickly seized the opportunity to ask Daddy what the colored people sought after, exactly. He reflected quietly for a moment, then softly replied, "They want more of what we've got. Most of them have never had a chance to get ahead in life."

He paused a moment or two longer and continued, "Our ancestors always worked hard to get ahead. Their ancestors were mostly slaves, and never had a chance to build a better life. They just want that chance."

PART 3:   INSTANT INTEGRATION

1966:

After years of fierce white resistance, new law mandated that public schools in Georgia were to be integrated with the coming of the new school year in Fall. Although there had been a Federal mandate to this effect for all states since 1954, it took twelve years for it to be forced through the Georgia legislature and school boards.

Though the battle had been long and hard, activists, both black and white, had prevailed, and now suddenly schools would become racially mixed overnight. Centuries of social separation would be instantly nullified. Some moderates called for gradual or systematic integration. But what came was an all-out thrusting together of polar opposites, and it felt a bit unnatural in many respects.

So many derogatory statements had filled the air for the last year, to the effect that "it was morally wrong" and "this would ruin our nation and wipe out our culture and eventually our race," that a young white boy, though benevolent by nature, could not entirely escape the sense that this historic event could be damaging. At best, it was sure to be awkward at first, if not catastrophic. *Were the youth of one generation to bear the burden of instantly erasing centuries of status quo?* Everyone in my school and community seemed to feel awkward about the general expectation of having their world immediately and drastically altered forever. Still, I could not suppress an element of adventure. After all, we were in the front lines of what the news media were falling all over. Whatever course it took, it was sure to be a new sort of thrill and daring.

For the first time, the subject of race was beginning to be more openly discussed in our home. Basically my parents were astonished, but optimistic. They gave us kids tidbits of advice that were generally compassionate, such as "When it comes, just be polite. That is the main thing.

WHITE BOY IN THE COLORED SECTION

You don't have to worry about anything. Just stand back and watch, and see how things go. Remember, they have feelings too," etc.

As my eighth grade year had rolled to a close, teachers had said less and less about the integration issue within earshot of the students. But one could readily discern the serious buzz going on amongst the teachers themselves. I could only assume they were gearing up for this new tidal wave, heretofore entirely unexpected and assumed impossible, yet now crashing onto the shores of their lives and careers with irreversible power. The sands of time were eroding.

But many students were voicing loud complaints about it with increasing frequency, especially the big bullies who sat in the back of the school bus and habitually bellowed anyway. I recall many remarks such as, "My Daddy says once they take over our schools, they'll be wantin' to swim with us at the City Pool, and go to our restaurants and movies!" and "Some people wanna hand everything over to them n_______rs for free! And it looks like the government's gonna just give them everything we got!"

For years we would daily meet a school bus full of black kids on Kingston Highway, headed toward their school in Rome as we went on out to ours. Sometimes our kids would wave or make funny faces with them. I can recall perhaps only one black boy daring enough to return a funny face at the white kids; overt expressions by blacks simply weren't done in our world. Most of the kids on our bus would make a darting, subtle glance toward them, in observance of the novelty of merely seeing a busload of colored kids for three or four seconds. It was almost as if segregation had been containerized, mobilized, and displayed for a few fleeting moments.

In retrospect, an awful lot was being said in the simple act of meeting another bus on the roadway. Segregation was thriving within every cell and fiber of our existence, and to suddenly endeavor to remove it was not too unlike a traumatic amputation, followed by grafting on a new alien limb. Who had caused all this, anyhow? Why was it up to us children to deal with it?

After a summer filled with worried conversations about "our white children having to mix with coloreds in the Fall," it finally happened. Our busses were still segregated the first week—the only attempt at gradual integration. But when the buses pulled up in front of our high school that first day, there it all was: a picture from living history which shall never erase itself from the chalkboard of my mind—a crowd of white kids and a crowd of black kids, standing apart and pondering what was to come next as we waited for the school doors to open. It seemed as momentous as Columbus discovering America, except in this case he had dragged all of the Old World with him, and now the continents came crashing together.

Yet it was silent, courteous, and almost serene. Only a trace of real apprehension could be felt drifting through the assemblage. From the black students' faces and mannerisms I saw more than ever just how like us they were. Were their concerns just like ours as well? And though the white world felt the blacks were wanting to conquer and seize our domain, these kids seemed just as apprehensive and uncertain as we were. Though no one in the white world was probably considering it, the blacks, too, were having their world ripped up by the roots and replanted suddenly into an alien realm. Yet had everyone been given the parental counsel to be polite, stand back, and observe? Apparently so. The entire scenario felt more exciting than ominous.

I had only spoken with black kids once in my life, some two years prior when Stephen and I made temporary playmates at the housing projects. We had achieved a "first" at that time. Now it was about to happen again. What happened next in my life was neither contrived nor planned nor even slightly expected. It simply happened. But I did it: I was the first white student at our high school to make friends with a black student, or to even speak to one.

It started by sheer accident. I was standing on the periphery of the white group, and on the black sideline was George Askew. He was perky and brimming with personality, which he found difficult to suppress. Yet he was as calm and courteous as one could expect. I'm not exactly sure how we struck up a conversation; it just happened, as would occur with boys anywhere. I do recall his looking toward the football practice field and mentioning how he was going to be a football star for our school. I wondered how much ball he had played: I was sure that his school did not have a football program below high school, for who would they play? What black schools were within driving distance, and how would they obtain funding to support young leagues? Yet George was confident, as evidenced by his earnest words, "I'm gonna show 'em. I'm gonna play football like a pro, and show 'em all."

I was suddenly moved by his stated desire to achieve. From what I had always heard, blacks had no drive nor motivation. How wrong that was. Centuries of pent-up social frustration now emerged in a fourteen year old boy's verbalized dream of playing football in a big way. How many other big dreams did he have? "Oh my, the black boy has wants and dreams. He is an American boy, just like me!" I thought. I replied, "Yeah, I'm gonna play. I've been playing for years."

George grinned faintly and stared at me a moment, then moved the subject on to wondering how hard high school was going to be, how the lunches might fare, and general fluff. No other white-black interactions seemed to be taking place. Some kids from both groups eyed us with casual curiosity. There was no sense at all that there would be any overt animosity between us. Yet the mystery lingered on. The first day was one of intense observation, as we were given class assignments, chose desks in our rooms, etc. There was some natural tendency of both races to gravitate toward "their own kind" in regard to seating. I have to hand it to the faculty: they were steady handed and fair in all their actions, including calling on students with no apparent awareness of racial difference. Indeed, they presented a calming effect which smoothed the acute slamming together of heretofore opposite worlds.

For the first week of school, we still rode segregated busses. The routes were not integrated until the second week. Now I was no longer watching to see the black bus every morning as I had done for years, but was actually riding with those kids. Two worlds had collided! When this happens, the worlds either shatter into drifting fragments, or become one. If mutually absorbing, there are major changes, beginning on the surface and then penetrating the depths. Elements exchange and often form new compounds.

Another novelty was that our new bus route was taking us through neighborhoods I had never seen before. Most of the blacks on my bus lived on Moran Lake Road, off Kingston Highway. It was very rural. The people dwelled in old houses of weathered, unfinished wood. There was likewise an old unpainted wooden church on one side of the road, and across from it stood a cinder-block tavern called the Fraternal Lounge. Our bus would go straight out that country road, pick up the Askews and others, turn around, and come straight back out. We also had the county's first woman bus driver, such an unprecedented event that her picture and story were featured in the newspaper. Funny how we students' social, racial, and educational world could make the most drastic changes since the continental drift, and the local paper not mention it; not grist for the mill of life. She was bigger news.

The scene went down much like it did passing each other in the halls at school. The whites observed furtively while the blacks got on and sat in silence. After a couple of days they began to talk softly among themselves. The white kids felt just as self-conscious as did they, and we never had an unkind incident one toward another. The blacks would climb on board and find a seat, the whites would take notice, and then would go on about their conversations. Within a week of riding together, the black kids were becoming outgoing and moderately expressive amongst themselves, seemingly jubilant to an extent, likely stemming from a sense of achievement and social progress. The initial tension was off their shoulders. Things were pretty much going their way—at least on the bus and at school. In the real world, the specter of racism was still raising its menacing head; but to an observable extent, we school kids were beginning to deal with it—finding a new path through it.

Thus within our microcosm, an air of relief gradually began to breathe upon us. White and black students seemed to be growing accustomed to one another's presence, passing each other in the corridors with no observable tension. Yet the first few weeks passed by without much social interaction to speak of. The leveling ground was P.E. We had to share the locker room and showers, exercise together, and play sports together. After our workouts, the white boys would hurry to the showers. The black boys seemed to dawdle and wait for a turn, after the white boys had toweled off and gotten dressed. This entire scenario was as novel to the blacks as it was to us, and they still were not accustomed to moving in and staking out their territory, at least amongst us. This had long been a white school; they came from a black school across the county. They were slowly beginning to fit in where once they did not belong. But whites and blacks were not ready to shower together.

Yet while students were still basically hanging loose and silently observing each other from a distance, George proved to be the social catalyst that thawed the iciest of walls. He was simply confident, cheery, and unafraid. He liked life, and the people in it. And he was poor. He lived in one of the poorest sections the county has ever known, but he was rich in spirit.

Soon some of the other white boys were joshing around with George, or smiling when he related his infinite supply of anecdotes and witty observations. I was proud that I had been the first to befriend poor, happy George, for now he was gaining popularity. He was a stocky boy who resembled a young Louie Armstrong, only handsomer. He had no cultural or intellectual cards to play; he was simply a friendly, happy fellow. I grew in amazement at how "normal" he seemed to feel in a world that had beaten his people down into a contrived state of inferiority. Except for George. George was unsinkable. Thanks to George, I could only imagine the achievements blacks could have made had they never been civilly suppressed.

One week Coach Tuggle had the class do a rotation of wrestling. Boys were carefully matched by height and weight, and I was assigned to wrestle against George. Another social first. Whenever it was our turn, we assumed the Half-Nelson position, and went at it. George was fast and clever. Though we were evenly matched, sometimes he got me in a hold I could not break. I found that in this situation, the technique to apply was tickling. A quick tickle to his belly, and he would come apart, roll away, and erupt in laughter. It never made him angry.

Later in the day I would occasionally overhear white boys saying to others, "Did you hear? Turner had to wrestle with a colored boy!" Sometimes another might interject, "Yeah, but it was just old George. He's all right."

George and I would always smile and say hello when changing classes, or perhaps chat a moment or two while waiting for a room to open. But as for sitting and socializing, that still seemed out of the question—until one day I just went and sat by him and some other black students on the school steps during break, and chatted. The others either smiled briefly, or looked away with embarrassment. None seemed particularly to mind me, but showed no interest in talking with me. But George, bless him, could not have cared less about the oddity of the situation, and talked with me anyway.

I would usually let George open a topic, and just follow along. He was so cock-sure of himself and always had an opinion about everything. Soon we were buzzing along about cars or teachers or sports, oblivious to the world. But on this day I did not appear oblivious to others, it seems. Or at least, not to one redneck bully in twelfth grade who gave me a menacing glare as he walked by our little gathering. He ambled along about twenty yards and leaned back against a brick wall, one foot propped up behind him, just watching me. He was readily noticeable by his "uniform," more appropriate for casual wear in the 1950's: tight jeans, white t-shirt with sleeves rolled up, waxed crewcut, and black engineer boots with large taps on the heels. When I sauntered on toward my next class, he called out to me, "Hey. Yeah, you! You turnin' n_______r on us, or somethin'?"

A cold nauseous feeling shot through me as I mozied on by. Turning red with embarrassment, I shook my head "no."

"Then remember where you came from, boy. Our old school was white country! This here ain't nuthin' but Jigaboo Junction, and yore gonna git yore self tore up if you go jumpin' the fence and join the black sheep!"

I had not heard overt ranting such as he spewed at me, for some time. Old hatreds die hard. But he was riding the race train for as far as it would go. Within two weeks he committed the only act of racial violence our high school ever witnessed. No one knows exactly how it got started, but he picked a fight with George's older brother, Eli.

Eli Askew was as kind and gentle a soul as I can ever recall meeting. Courteous to everyone, it was inconceivable how he could garner even the tamest of enemies. As with George, his lack of scholarly leanings or social status were no handicap to him. His genuine warmth and sense of kindness won him the same in return. And though he was the quieter of the two brothers, they shared a common talent for liking people and being liked.

But he and the redneck senior sure enough ended up in a fight. It was noised all over campus how Eli had managed to seize him in a headlock, and rammed his head into the side of a parked car. The ruffian left school that day, never to return. He had been shamed beyond repair, and chose to end his schooling then and there. In a way I felt sorry for him, and how he had wrecked his life. I likewise felt sympathy for Eli, who would surely never have hurt a flea, yet who had obviously been dealt an extreme, undeserved malice. Mostly I was glad the bully was gone, and would not likely be around to harass me.

Thankfully this incident of black-and-white violence involved someone as well accepted as Eli, and that the fight occurred well after the initial trial of two racial entities being thrust together. It speaks volumes for Eli's humble character that, although astonishment abounded over the unprecedented inner-racial duel, no one expressed rage or even displeasure toward Eli. He was a golden soul and everyone but the anachronistic bully could appreciate that.

Now another question emerged. If the gentlest of black souls could rise up and fight for himself as Eli had done, what were the rest of them capable of doing? What did they want? Were they planning to attack whites? Did they really, as some had commented, want to "take over?" There was no history of a black ever engaging a white in physical strife in Rome, Georgia, and Eli's fight may well have been the first bodily combat between a white and a black since the founding of Floyd County.

Only a few weeks prior, the incident would have been seized upon by many constituents of the white populace, who would have blamed the incident entirely upon Eli, and might have reigned with terror against blacks across the county and perhaps the region. The incident being a small and private affair, its news passing only from mouth to ear by students, lacked any significant information upon which to build a meaningful account. There were no admitted witnesses; Eli went on smoothly with his school attendance without a word on the subject; and if the faculty knew anything, they kept mum. Still, it was nothing short of a miracle that the little episode did not explode into massive violence.

It is a credit to the white students in general that no one railed against Eli, nor sought revenge. Yet of course most of the whites still looked upon the blacks as a social oddity, and did not necessarily mingle. Such is the paradox of wanting to be fair, yet apart. It has likely always been an integral factor within the white collective unconscious, and perhaps still is to an appreciable degree.

The story soon died down, surprisingly. Surely part of it had to do with many white students having known this bully for years, and his reputation for the grossest of behavior. Still, the imagery of it all resonated through my thoughts for a considerable time. And now a new image was approaching through the haze, ever attempting to focus itself; or was it I who was trying to bring it into focus? My subconscious must have been working overtime to suppress a concept that had been taboo for centuries: that the black people may not want to "stay in their place." They may not want to remain mired down in societal restraint. They might well be on the verge of breaking out, and apparently the desire *had been there all along.*

Integration was alive and in the air, borne aloft by the circulating winds of human tradition that never changed. Whites of every class were increasingly discussing the subject, expressing awe and wagging their heads in disbelief at how things were changing. But to date, it was us students, white and black, who were doing the changing, feeling the changes, and ultimately making the changes. There was a very long road ahead. Some signs of white dominance in the educational system would linger for years. Since I began school in 1958, all Department of Education films shown in Georgia schools had the same opening credits music: "Dixie," played rapidly as the credits rolled. In the background was the State flag bearing the Confederate battle emblem. All school films would be presented this way until long after I finished public school.

As sensitive as I was to the plight and feelings of black students, I never conceived there would come a time when "Dixie" would be ridiculed and abandoned. Like most whites, I never thought of it as reflecting prejudice. To me, it was just a pretty tune about a place called Dixieland, the same tune Lincoln had the band play at the White House when the Confederacy surrendered, as a gesture of goodwill. There is nothing in the lyrics to suggest slavery or bigotry or white supremacy. Yet to this day I can never recall hearing a black person whistle the tune. Only with prolonged thought on the subject did I conclude that yes, perhaps blacks do considerate it a Confederate rallying song, and not one about regional pride. This rousing song, once heard prominently across the South, is pretty much "gone with the wind."

TURNER

I remember riding in the countryside and sometimes seeing large cotton farms. Most of it was still picked by hand back then. The machines were not yet widely accepted, partly because they left about half the crop in the field. So hand-picking was still considered the most efficient harvest modality at the time. Or perhaps it was the cheap wages that held the system in place for so long. After all, though we were preparing to send men to the moon, farms near us were not buying combine machines to harvest the cotton crops.

As if peering back in time, one could look out in those fields and see black people picking the stuff, as they always had. I never personally saw a white person picking cotton. The black laborers would drag their long white canvas bags along, strapped across their shoulders, and work along just as in olden times. It was an anachronistic novelty to see blacks had never left the cotton fields of Georgia, a century after the Civil War ended. George and Eli Askew had picked cotton since boyhood.

Everyday terms and expressions still permeated the language of the white culture. A common insult when admonishing someone not to touch something was to say, "Get your cotton pickin' hands off of that!" Picking cotton *per se* does not get one's hands dirty. The implication was that the hands of those who picked cotton were those of an inferior class of people. Nevertheless, the phrase had become such an everyday saying, that one did not consciously register what it meant originally. It was just a thing whites said, though careful analysis will illustrate that it has its roots deep in the times when blacks were considered less than respectable. It is nonetheless commendable that whites were usually sensitive enough not to use the expression in the presence of blacks, revealing that indeed it was symptomatic of racial prejudice.

We did not have segregated drinking fountains in the school. An oversight, or just a budget shortcoming? They were there to serve all. But black students tended to bypass them when whites were near, to avoid being seared by disapproving eyes. If a black did drink from a water fountain, a thirsty white would often wait to make certain no whites saw him drink after a black, then would furtively sneak a sip. Yet no overt discourtesy was being expressed by the whites toward the blacks. How could this be? How deep and long-running was the stream of racial bias that seeped into every aspect of white life, conscious or unconscious? Apparently it was as ancient as "Old Man River," and not soon to dry up.

Even obituaries were segregated! I was getting old enough to read the newspaper more closely now. One of my most surprising discoveries was that deceased black listings in the newspaper would have "Col." for "Colored," after their names in parentheses, as if for some reason the reader needed to know if the departed was black or not. I once rode my pony atop a wooded hill not far from our house, on a site that had once been a plantation. There amidst the towering oaks and rustling leaves being stirred about by my pony's hooves, I came upon an old family cemetery. Several of the names on the gravestones off to one side were followed by "Col." Thinking this stood for colonel, I was impressed at how many officers of high rank had been in this family. Then it slowly dawned on me like a low-voltage epiphany: these were colored people's graves! I sat awhile in the saddle marveling over this find. At least the white family who allowed them to be buried so near their kin had the decency to give them real engraved stones. But even in death, white people did not want to mingle with their "distant cousins of color."

I had been in the 4-H Club since sixth grade. To this day it is the best developer of youth and their talents of any program available in the schools. Perhaps this is because it operates independently from the school systems. Club meetings focus on its members growing into full, worthwhile citizens, pledging one's Head, Heart, Hands, and Health to the betterment of the community and the world. The members select a project area from among dozens of fields, be it technology, horsemanship, agriculture, leadership, home economics, sports, crafts, or many others. The member develops a five minute speech with manual demonstration on their project, presents it to the club, and qualifies to go on to county, district, state, and/or national competition.

They also hold superb summer camps which rival any camp program on earth, for a very nominal cost. Georgia has the largest and best developed 4-H camp resort in the world, so fine a place that many organizations hire it out for holding conventions in this beautiful retreat. I never thought about blacks not participating in 4-H in our county since they were not in our schools. It was not until I went off to county and district competition, and summer camp, that I realized they were not involved. Again, this did not particularly surprise me, being accustomed to living in a whites-only world.

Even when we integrated schools, we did not initially have blacks in our local club. But then came county competition in 1966, held in classrooms at a central high school on a Saturday. It was a surprise indeed to see a couple of black kids from another school show up in my competition room, the Home Gardening division. The biggest surprise was how poorly prepared they were. I was accustomed to our county extension office holding workshops for us, drilling us on our speeches and adding professional touches to our visual aids and posters.

The black kids had nothing of the sort. They could not have been more poorly prepared if they had been hypnotized, bound, gagged, and blindfolded. It was apparent that the county 4-H leaders were not visiting their schools, nor inviting them to their offices for competition tutoring. Finally the turn came for the first black kid. The judges managed to maintain stoic expressions in the face of what was, to them, an earth-shattering social conundrum.

A boy's name was called by one of the judges, and he strode to the desk with an uneasy smile. He had no materials, easel, or notes. He produced a sheet of notebook paper that was crayon-colored a brownish red on the top half, and black on the bottom. He proceeded to describe how he plants his potatoes with seeds, when actually this is done by planting pieces of potato in the soil bearing at least one "eye." He then held his paper with the reddish part up, and described it as the good top soil, and pointed to the black portion underneath as representing the less fertile subsoil, entirely opposite of the facts. The lead judge was struggling to conceal his bemusement, but managed to recompose himself. The boy had been robbed by a governmental agency his family supported with taxes, just as mine did. So much for "separate but equal."

I won the county Gardening competition that day. I rather felt I would, being so thoroughly prepared by my 4-H leaders. The black kids did not place at all, though it seemed very clear that the white judges had been fair to them, courteously asking them questions and offering words of encouragement following their presentations, as they did with all of us. My pride of winning was dampened by the pity I felt for those black kids, whose level of preparedness and attention was little short of social sabotage; or at best, severe neglect. Yet I can never forget the confidence that boy showed as he proudly presented to the white folks what was, to him, a milestone of achievement. He had stood forth and found a place amongst us—or despite us.

I was slowly beginning to see that this generation of blacks seemed more confident and ready to advance, than prior generations; and pronouncedly more so than the elderly blacks I had scared when sitting by them in the colored waiting room. Daniel Boone or Lewis and Clark would never have sent children ahead of them, to brave and conquer the unknown. But school children were in the front lines of the biggest social upheaval America had seen since emancipation. Had these black youth been prepared for these social trailblazing days by their parents? Or had the heavens chosen this time to bring forth their spirits for some great cause among their people? They seemed confident enough to take on whatever they were allowed to do, and apparently what these young people needed was merely opportunity. A wise old mother cat will remain aloof from the unknown, but her kittens, if unimpeded, will romp and explore cheerfully and fearlessly. Apparently this natural phenomenon has a broader human application, as well.

One such opportunity manifest itself in the form of football. I joined the junior varsity team and three black boys turned out. They were not the cowering stereotypes, either, though they were somewhat quiet and polite at first. But they had football in their eyes, and they were good players, too. Moreover, the coach allowed all three of them to play a great deal. Though nary a word was ever spoken about racial policy by the coach, by his actions he was able to implement fairness to them by leveling the field and treating all of us equally. (And he shouted at everyone equitably, too.) The black players did not hold back, either. I shared many fierce hits against one black lineman during practice, and I could see he was not afraid to slam bodies with white boys. So I felt it no disrespect to apply my years of experience against him, and hit him hard every time. He only respected me for it, and I him.

Most of the teams we played were from distant rural towns where blacks were scarcer. I do not recall ever coming up against a black opponent except in practice. I do call to mind a few statements by surprised spectators at a couple of games:

"Well, lookee yonder! They got colored boys on their team!" and "Can you imagine that, colored boys playin' agin our boys!"

It made me a little proud in a way. We were a novelty, our lineup was a first, and we were in town to whup those people's boys. None of the whites on our team—and they were some of the rowdiest rednecks on earth—ever showed discourtesy to our black players. I doubt they had told their families about playing with coloreds, because they also seemed surprised when they turned out for our games. But our focus was to win, and to accomplish same by teamwork. Nothing else mattered. The football field was indeed a good leveling ground.

These were social changes of great import, though the everyday world had not improved for the average black person. Poverty and lack of position still prevailed. There was a short cut for driving into Rome from the

WHITE BOY IN THE COLORED SECTION

Kingston Highway, which took you along a narrow street by the Etowah River, in the heart of the black urban slums. And slummy they were. This whole section of town was nothing but ancient-looking structures of bare wood, never having been painted. Many window spaces were covered with cardboard. One night as we drove to town, the door was open on one house, allowing me a brief glance at its interior. There was a single light bulb illuminating the fact that this house was entirely devoid of furniture, at least in the front room. Until that moment I had naturally assumed all houses had furniture. This one didn't even have a picture on the wall, nor glass in the covered-up windows.

My Mom owed a black woman three days' pay, for having substituted for Louise. We drove up a long dirt road out in the country a ways. It was rainy, but the tree canopy had kept the road from becoming mush. When we arrived at the woman's residence, I was surprised when Mom said it was her house; it looked more like a shed to me. It was clad in bare wood and rather Spartan in appearance. I was glad for the occupants' sake to at least see a wire overhead, bringing electric service to the dubious domicile.

Mom asked me to take the woman's money up to her door because there was mud all about the place. Compounding the messy scene was a huge trench cut just before the shanty, in which pipe was being laid. It was a muddy mess, and even for an athletic young lad, presented a fairly challenging jump to get across. It was several feet deep and about four feet across. I was wearing my best clothes, and durst not ruin them by falling into the quagmire. Moreover, there was no visible means of being rescued should I indeed plunge into the clutches of this muddy morass. I wondered how in the world this woman could get out and go places. With a running start, I did manage to hurl myself over the canal of mud.

I trudged around to the front of the shack and tapped on the door. A startled voice responded, "Who dat?"

"It's the Turners. I'm bringing some money for ___________________." The door pulled open slightly. A skeptical young black woman peered out at me, then on recognizing me, took the cash and thanked me. Just as quickly, the door was closed. It did not take a trained analytical eye to sum up the myriad factors at play in that scene, rendering it a social phenomenon of significant intensity.

Several factors impacted the discomfiture of this terse visit, the overriding aspect being the stark poverty. But within that poor structure existed a cellular nucleus, whose every component reflected arrested advancement. The interior walls were the same bare wood as the exterior, absent any insulation. The woman had a sister sharing the one-room dwelling. There was scarcely room for the two little cots.

There was no appreciable décor or bric-a-brac. The sister was clad only in her slip as she ironed her work dress. There were perhaps three garments apiece on hangers suspended on a cord running along one wall. I could see little motive for hope or aspiration within this cramped little world, yet therein was a woman ironing an outfit so she could get to work. What kept her going?

Other than a small old radio, there was nothing by way of entertainment or pursuit of life's enjoyments. There was no refrigerator, and only a little hotplate for heating food. There was no telephone: as domestic workers, they obtained occasional employment by word of mouth. Employers would have to drive up that dirt road to pick them up, or they might have to walk two or three miles. Over the years I wondered if they were still semi-existing within the confines of that oversized woodshed. Yet the memory that stands out above all is how neat and clean the place was kept inside. The element of pride did exist within their hearts, if only miniscule in its reach.

Then there was the stark contrast between their milieu, and the out-of-place image I presented to them: my status as a well-dressed white boy with money in his hand, a nice car to leave in, and a decent house to go home to. And a future to look forward to. Our acute, glaring differences hit me in an instant and was over in a flash, yet has seared a lasting memory in my mind that has never waned. Again, pangs of pity and disbelief whizzed around in my head as we drove home, knowing there were no barricades to my chances for a bright future, while these women and countless others like them merely existed day to day. They had no A to Z. It was A to B, and sometimes just A.

As the 1967-1968 school year rolled along, the racial mix seemed to grow more natural. The bus rides were low-stress, and occasionally whites and blacks would converse in a friendly manner. The real advances were being made now on television, at least on the variety shows. These were showcases of talent much akin to the old vaudeville and radio days. Quite a number of black entertainers were being featured, and well accepted. It was as though entertaining whites was a natural calling for blacks, as my Grandpa used to say. This may have seemed partially true since few blacks could afford a television set, to really appreciate the stardom of members of their race. But naturally the whole show-biz scene was a boon to blacks in general. Still, they were not showing up on other TV programs such as sitcoms and dramas. That would imply social mingling, and the white world was not ready for that yet.

Who couldn't like Sammy Davis, Jr.? Or Lena Horne? And now many pro sports figures were rising to prominence among the blacks. Distinguished among these were Hank Aaron, hero of our Atlanta Braves. Mr. Aaron was bringing much pride to the South by his remarkable performance on the baseball field, though reportedly there were some whites who sent him and other black stars hate mail. Whenever a black would stand out in news coverage, many whites would grumble about them getting so much attention. And white adults were more frequently discussing the "black situation," marveling aloud over the social changes brought about by school integration; and now, slowly, within entertainment and sports venues.

I was about to sidestep the scene, come Fall. My parents approved my transferring to a private "whites only" boarding school. This was not done for purposes of segregation, but for the academic and cultural environment. The Academy was not touted as being segregated; it was just a given. There was a subtle line in the application form that indicated the admissions process was "culturally selective." It was so delicately stated, in fact, that I had to ask Mom what it meant. She replied that only whites were admitted. I harkened back to her having to explain the "whites only" sign at the laundromat when I was a child. This time I merely shrugged it off, thinking about how much I was going to enjoy the Academy, where Martin and other kin had attended. It was classy and prestigious and that was all I really thought about at this juncture.

Mom took me to the finest clothing store in Rome, Esserman's, where I got outfitted with some very fine clothes, and was particularly proud of the double-breasted navy blue blazer. A blue blazer and gray slacks were required wear at the Academy. I was going to hit campus in style.

There were no blacks anywhere, except for a lone fellow who worked on the campus maintenance crew. "Old Carl" they called him. He was quiet and unsophisticated, the kind white organizations liked to hire for menial jobs, and was focused on nothing but his manual labor. In time I would come to see Old Carl become the subject of some racist boys' uncalled-for taunting and scheming, but for now he did not enter my realm of existence; I was concentrated on beginning a new school year within an entirely new world.

The Academy was preppy, but not all the students were. There was actually a good assortment of class backgrounds; bright academics, and lesser lights. They were all white, too, it seemed, until all the Fall 1967 students had arrived. Among them was one Native American boy from North Carolina everyone called Cherokee. He fit right in. In the East, Native Americans are more accepted and even revered than in some other parts of the nation, even though most whites never see or meet any.

Soon I met another "Indian," or so I thought. We struck up a conversation. He was dressed as if he, too, had been on a spree through Esserman's; sharp attire. From the quality of his wardrobe, one almost didn't notice how he walked with a slight limp, and had a withered arm. As it happened, his father owned a high class clothing store and kept him supplied with the finest wardrobe I had ever seen. He was slightly darker in his complexion and had black hair, and I assumed he, too, was of Native American descent. He was quiet and polite. His name was Joel. Joel and I spoke for a minute or two before I asked, "Where ya from?"

"North Carolina," he answered softly, through a faint smile. "Raleigh."

"So, are you a Cherokee? We have a Cherokee boy here from North Carolina."

He chuckled lightly and replied, "No. I'm Jewish."

I had never met a Jew personally. Within my narrow scope of life, I did not even know there were Jews in America. I knew nothing about them. I had never heard of them in school, or on TV. Though Jews had been in Georgia for ages, they simply were not mentioned. I was entirely ignorant of their presence and contribution to society. I didn't realize Mr. Esserman was Jewish. I didn't even know what it meant to be Jewish.

I was in one of those unexpected situations where life had dropped my mind onto a whirling merry-go-round, stirring me up with confusion. But they were around. Georgia had had a Jewish community since its earliest Colonial days. Other than the *Bible*, my only association with Jews was a brief recollection of an article I had partially read about a Jewish woman surviving some kind of a mass execution, and how she was able to escape. The whole story was confusing to me, since it was not a common topic within the constrictive confines of my little world.

A brash bully from Florida noticed my new togs and remarked, "Not bad slacks, Turner. Where'd ya get 'em?"

"From a store in Rome, Georgia, called Esserman's," I replied with a sense of sophistication.

"Oh, the Jew-joint. *Rabbi* Esserman's place!" Joel alerted on the remark.

"The what?"

"It's owned by Rabbi Esserman," the boor went on. Mr. Esserman had waited on me personally. He was the most distinguished and finest dressed gentleman I had ever seen in town. At the time I did not know he was Jewish, or that Jews even resided in Rome. In fact, all I knew about Jews at age fourteen was that they featured prominently in the *Bible*, and there was some sorry business between them and the Nazis which I did not comprehend. It was not talked about or mentioned on TV or movies, or in text books, so naturally I knew nary a thing about them. All I knew was, I had met two of them, and decided they were nice people. "Did he drool and wring his hands whenever he saw your money? Ha ha!" I didn't get it. Joel sat speechless. I detected a slight pooling of moisture in his eyes. I was witnessing for the first time an entirely new dimension of prejudice; new to me, anyway.

I soon discovered that Joel had a social handicap. He was both intelligent, and yet intellectually uncoordinated. He could begin a conversation with seeming sophistication, but would wander and grow simple in his grasp. He was also very gullible, and once the bully and his two cohorts comprehended this, they made maximal manipulation of his suggestible state. Sometimes they would scare him into thinking he had a dread disease, or that a Jew-killer was on the loose, and he would tremble with panic. On realizing he was being tricked, he would fly into a rage, which seemed to bring the bullies even more delight.

Their antics became sophisticated. Three or so of them would agree in advance to mention the same frightening lie to him throughout the day, confirming in his mind that it was perhaps true. The lead bully might pass him in the dorm, stop with a jolt of feigned shock, and remark, "Hey, you look like you have radiation sickness! Have you been sitting too close to your radiator? You'll be lucky if you live another day!" Joel would walk away quietly perplexed. After a series of like encounters throughout the day with the tormentors, Joel would grow so paranoid he would wheeze and gasp and fly around like a mad hen.

One of the boys might say, "Joel, you'd better get up to the dispensary and see the nurse! There might be time to save your life!" Joel would rush up to the nurse's station and we would not see him for the rest of the day. He could sometimes be glimpsed lying on the clinic cot, apparently under sedation.

On field trips, the bully squad would sing anti-Jewish songs on the bus which they had made up, or duck-march up and down the aisle in Nazi fashion, as Joel would tremble and weep. If he would not fly into a tirade against them, they would soon tire of their torturous antics and quieten down. Most boys were afraid to stand up for Joel for fear of being picked on themselves, though occasionally an upperclassman might smile and make a half-cocked remark such as, "Leave the poor little Jew-boy alone! He's had enough—for today."

There was one boy in our dorm some called "The Twisted Genius." He slipped into Joel's room and placed a speaker beneath his bed, and ran the wire out the window, and up to his room. The latter stood out from the façade of the building at an angle, allowing him to look down into Joel's room. At night he would utter scary sounds and threats over a microphone, which could be heard through the hidden speaker.

The spooky voice would moan out words such as, "Joel! This is the ghost of the dorm of doom! I died in this room! If you do not get up and turn on your light, you will die, too!" The evildoer would later boast through his haughty laughter how he had seen Joel's light quickly come on, and soon he would dart about the room in panic. "I'm going to work on post-hypnotic suggestion next," he concluded. We believed him.

Joel spent a good deal of time in the headmaster's office, crying and seeking a solution to his dilemma. Things got so bad, that eventually our biology teacher allowed him to stand up and read a report on the history of Judaism, both ancient and modern. It was so obviously out of place for a science class that it actually seemed to garner some serious attention. But soon things were back to normal: torment the pitiable handicapped lad to the point of frenzy. Those boys who did not care about his being a Jew, but still liked to make fun of a person who was awkward both physically and mentally, supplied a softer yet continual atmosphere of rejection and annoyance.

The situation became so difficult for Joel that its foul redolence had risen to the nostrils of the Academy administration on an increasingly frequent basis. Resultantly, a special evening presentation was arranged in connection with the issue. We had monthly "fireside chats" on Sunday evenings in the dining hall on a variety of uplifting subjects. But this particular evening was a first. At the faculty table sat the guest speaker: Mr. Esserman!

Rabbi Esserman was a most congenial and dashing gentleman. No one could possibly dislike him. He smiled throughout his presentation. Having known only one Jew, but having heard countless unfavorable remarks against them as a people, it was refreshing to see a confident, well-constituted Jewish man for a change. His topic, surely a historical first at the Academy or anywhere within the region, was on the origins and culture of Judaism. The students seemed to get the message: no more anti-Semitism. Joel continued to get teased and disrespected, though it was less about his religious preference than his handicaps, which some ill-bred boys continued to find amusing. But the underlying factor was prejudice. Though I had never thought of Joel as being racially that distinct, it was the same far-spreading monster than had caused blacks so much suffering: an inability to accept difference.

I wasn't hearing much mention of blacks anymore; they simply were not around. But two students who had part-time jobs on the campus maintenance crew liked to joke over their accounts of having played Old Carl for a fool. He was so quiet and docile, there is no way anyone could find reason to harass him—except that he was black in a totally white world.

"Ha ha, we got Old Carl today!" one of the perpetrators scoffed. "We were taking a break. Two of us were running around with buckets of water, pretending to try and splash each other. Then one of us pretended to trip, right in front of Old Carl, letting his water splash on his feet! Ha ha, it was perfect. But Old Carl just sat there and smiled, kind of nervous like."

"Why, that's about his speed," replied another. "Imagine if he was to do that to you? What'd ya do then?"

"Why, I'd give that *n______r* the beating of his life!"

Another time the boy bragged, "I was directing Old Carl while he was backing up the dump truck. Made him back into a big tree, and man you should have seen him jump out, all scared! Nearly turned white! Then when he saw what happened, he got scared looking and got back in the truck. Never said a word!"

But Old Carl, like any man, could only take so much. I was walking along a campus path when the grounds crew truck rolled by. One of the older white boys riding in back was goading a younger one to holler a racial insult at Old Carl. Apparently he was willing to perform this crude act in order to gain social points with an upperclassman. I heard him yell, "Carl, slow down, you stupid old *n______r*!"

Old Carl hit the brakes, the truck surged forth with inertia, and the second it swayed back to a stop Carl was already on the ground. He looked to be in a rage. He stormed around to the back of the truck and, shaking with anger, blurted out, "Who done called me dat? Who done called me a stupid—*somethin'-or-'nuther?*" He couldn't bring himself to say the word. That would be overly confrontational.

The boys were aghast. None of us had ever seen an angry black, and no one knew what to expect next. The grounds supervisor, Pop, drove up at the same instant and got out of his car, looking puzzled as he approached the scene.

"What's happening, fellers?" Pop asked. No replies. "Carl, why'd you stop?"

Carl was the very picture of hurt and shame, rolled together. With a downward glance and some trepidation he managed to answer, "Somebody called me a stupid black somethin'-or-'nuther." He could not look Pop in the face, despite having just bared his teeth at the boys. Carl knew he was now out of his element, and it was hurtful to see him slipping back into the docile role to which he was accustomed.

Pop paled a moment, then asked, "Which one was it, Carl?"

Carl pointed at the culprit and said, "Dat one right dere. He de one done said it."

Pop called to the boy, "You need to come over here and apologize to Carl, and shake hands." It was like a playground admonition by a kindergarten teacher.

The boy looked sickly as he stumbled over to Carl and said, "I'm sorry, Carl. It just—well—I didn't mean to say it." I think that beneath the boy's fright and humiliation, there might have actually been a strand of regret at hurting innocent Old Carl. There had certainly been no call for it. He was prodded into it by an older boy who thought it would be fun. But it obviously was not fun to Carl, and I think all those present learned a deeply burning lesson that day.

As Carl climbed back into the cab, Pop said to the boys, "Fellers, things are changing. We have LBJ to thank for that. 'Cause the time is coming when you'll have to put up with a lot more from the colored people, and there ain't a thing can be done about it. So you might as well start gettin' used to it."

I sauntered on my way, entirely absorbed by the incident. Not only had a black man actually stood up to white tormentors, one of the most classically passive and compliant ones had erupted as if to say, "We don't like where you've put us. We want more. We want change!" The prospect was both humiliating and frightening. I couldn't resist feeling some shame for what the white race had done to the blacks, with centuries of suppression and abuse now being manifest through Old Carl. And yet the prospect for an uprising was frightening. Many whites claimed there would be an upheaval one day, and I stressed over the possibility. Why couldn't it work out more smoothly?

WHITE BOY IN THE COLORED SECTION

As in times past, I reflected on evidences I had seen of black people exhibiting through subtle behavior that they were people too, with the same needs and same desire for dignity. Again and again this epiphany would resound in my mind, and each time I would further resolve to never hurt a black person, or those of any other race. Still, in the recesses of my mind lurked a trace of that generations-old desire to have things the white way, to not have to sway to the approaching black winds of change.

It never occurred to me that such a viewpoint may be hypocritical. To want to be fair and kind, while also having one's own world intact, seemed perfectly normal. Concessions most feared by white adults were blacks having political or economic power, and thus power over whites. Students sometimes complained about other schools having blacks on their sports or debate teams. Most whites in general did not want to share a social life with people of color, regardless of whether they felt superior to them or equal. The paradox of benign prejudice was so deep-rooted within the white psyche, it may never be fully weeded out.

The general consensus was that "they just want to take over." Indeed, though black students seemed to enjoy competing at mostly-white sporting or scholastic events, it did not seem to me that they felt joy in taking over white turf. They just seemed to be glad for the opportunity to function within a meaningful setting just like other kids, to feel worthwhile and viable. Yet warnings of their "encroachment" were filling the air. Other than news reports from the TV and magazines, it was not so obvious at the Academy, which was a white-washed world. But news media were, indeed, beginning to cover the topic of race increasingly, until the subject was becoming a daily issue.

1968:

1968 exploded with many new types of music and musical groups. Pop music had long reigned and was taking on exciting new dimensions, and now Soul and the Motown Sound were just as big, and widely enjoyed. Country and Western almost went out of business as these styles made their meteoric rise. There soon got to be a division within the dorm between Pop and Psychedelic, and Soul. Students would gravitate to one room or another to hear the latest records, while a friendly sort of rivalry became evident. One either identified with the Rock or Psychedelic crowd, or Soul Music fans.

Some of the new Soul sounds were absolutely fascinating, and gave me shivers. Sometimes a boy would pass my dorm room while my radio was on, and tease me about "going for that monkey music." This phenomenon was helping bridge the vast chasm between white and black kids. It was beginning to happen in the 1950's with Rhythm-n-Blues, as white teens were beginning to discover black radio stations and secretly listen to them. Before long the black artists were being featured on white teen TV shows. But the bridge began to sag as record producers started remaking some black hits, using white singers. Now in 1968 the world seemed like a musical festival of many unique styles, so much so that it was difficult to classify them under narrow labels. But Soul was getting under my skin, and would lead to my following the re-discovery of Blues by and by. It became a part of me, and changed me forever.

More civil unrest involving blacks was being reported, but it did not affect us at the Academy. But the day Martin Luther King was assassinated changed everything, etching its ominous and far-reaching specter into the public psyche forever. It came as a big shock to everyone, but within a short time some Academy students were beginning to make degrading remarks about the man and "his kind," a few of the rowdier ones even celebrating King's passing. Soon the entire affair seemed to have a mild festival spirit about it.

By the day of King's funeral and national day of mourning, several of the students decided to wear wacky get-ups, laughingly donning anything that appeared funky or out of order. "Dressing like *n______*rs for National N______r Day," some were heard to say. One teacher even came to school sporting an imitation leopard skin blazer and beret, and funky sunglasses. The scene was so disruptive that the dean announced over lunch that anyone wearing inappropriate attire would be punished. The festive spirit died down and life got back to normal. But on the TV news there were many stories about blacks rioting in major cities. Chaos ensued, and there was much loss of life and property. Although Atlanta authorities took security precautions over anticipated violence in the inner city, we never heard of any trouble in Georgia.

Ironically, it was about this time that our biology teacher, who was also the track coach, shocked my class with a statement no one seemed to believe was coming from his own mouth. He laid it out plainly, "I almost wish the Academy would admit some colored students, to enhance our track team." He began to draw a lower leg on the chalk board and continued, "You see, here is the calf muscle as it appears on a colored person's leg. High, like that. When the calf muscle is high up, it makes the leg move faster and of course makes the person a faster runner." Then he resumed his lecture on anatomy and physiology.

The remainder of the class time was the quietest ever witnessed. Glancing around at the other boys' faces revealed they were all in an apparent state of shock and reflection. I couldn't believe the coach's words myself. And though I secretly thought it noble of him to find some good in black people, I felt it a little irresponsible to blurt it out like that in a segregated school. I also felt a twinge of jealousy over his suggesting blacks were generally faster runners than whites.

His timing may have been awkward by coinciding with MLK's death, but it was spot-on with regard to the racial openness now gradually swelling the air. All the nation was having to stop and take notice of what had happened, and tragic as it was, Dr. King's work had not halted. It was marching on with renewed fervor. The word was out now. The hounds were loosed. Blacks were moving in strength, more than ever, toward major societal changes. Occasionally white racists stepped up their attacks on blacks, and in several cities blacks were demonstrating and sometimes attacking whites. Many feared it was the beginning of a civil war, or race revolt.

Many civil rights leaders took to the public forefront and pleaded for blacks and whites alike to heed the peaceable teachings of Dr. King, which seemed to have contributed to a general calming of tensions. Until now, Dr. King was seen by most whites as an incidental sideshow of sorts, an outspoken colored man who needed quieting. It was unforeseeable that he would one day be included in school history books, and a national holiday would be named in his honor. For the moment, he was just another outspoken black figure who had come into national prominence by being ruthlessly killed, and white folks waited to see what would come of all this now.

Television can be largely attributed with smoothing the way for blacks to advance. For besides this medium stirring up animosity by constant coverage of racial strife, there were also many programs in which issues were beginning to be discussed within a positive vein, promulgating the need to respect their human and civil rights. It was slowly becoming public policy to eschew racist views and words, and a sense of shame was being projected into the air concerning any who would demean blacks. Racist jokes were still told, but on the quiet. Whites were beginning to glance around to see if any blacks were present, before making any degrading remarks, or even to say the word "black." It was no longer cool, at least in the public sense, to appear racist, though resentment and derogatory remarks were strong as ever.

Yet the old dog was slow to die. One day Dad and I listened to a preacher on the radio, as he spoke of some state of hypocritical corruption or another. He paused and commented, "Sounds to me like we have a colored man in the lumber business." I didn't get it. But Dad sure did! His expression was somewhere between shock and disbelief.

"What does that mean?" my voice piped out, revealing my naiveté.

Dad shook his head. "Can't believe he said that. He must think it is a nice way of saying 'There's a n_______r in *the wood pile!'"* I had never heard Dad use that word; he was only explaining to me what the preacher meant.

"Well, what does that mean?"

"It's an old saying that means there is something being covered up, like when a runaway slave would hide in a wood pile."

"Talk about your basic hypocrisy." Dad nodded at my words. Apparently for some, such as this preacher, the first step toward racial niceties was a watering-down of racial slurs.

I was becoming so immersed in Blues music that I began to identify with it. The music of Eric Burdon awakened me to its soul-stirring sound and feel. What a renaissance it was for me, a young white lad who had never really allowed any musical form to completely dominate his tastes. But Blues hit me like lightening, and it was like I had happened upon an old friend long lost. Blues was becoming to me the aegis under which I stood; my badge of identity. Martin had gone to the Marine Corps and left some records behind. I knew not to mess with them while he was around, but once he was enlisted, my curiosity got the best of me and I discovered a new world. I played his Animals albums over and over until I nearly wore them out. I could scarcely believe such soul-stirring music could exist within a pop form.

I was not a rocker exactly. In fact, I was one of the most conservative boys around. But I was drawn into the music of Eric Burdon and the Animals, and played it so often at the Academy, my dorm mates started calling me New Eric. There were other Blues groups gaining in popularity. Furtherance of my interest therein led to the discovery that *these white artists were actually replicating a black American music form that had died out in popularity before my musical awakening!*

I had to think about this phenomenon awhile: white British chaps were re-introducing black American music to the Americans, and we kids thought it was British music. Turns out it was largely based on the old R&B tunes of Chuck Berry, Bo Diddley, Little Richard, et al. Even the Beatles had gotten their start within that genre. Then Eric

Clapton and colleagues were building upon grassroots Bluesmen such as Muddy Waters, Howlin' Wolf, and John Lee Hooker.

When the true source of this music was revealed to me, I was at first surprised; then remembering the soulful performances of many black singers on TV, I began to secretly blend into the soul of it and felt that as long as I was hip to the scene, I was only digging the cool artistry of it all, and not deserting my race. Yes, I could see I had a twinge of racism within me; it exists within all people to some degree. But my lack of *malevolent* prejudice left my heart open to this magical music, and I wanted more. Racists in the dorm did not call the British Blues "n______r music," thinking it was of white origin. But anyone listening to Soul or Motown tunes was sometimes called a *n______r* lover.

I did overhear two maintenance employees complaining about such music they were overhearing while working in the dorm, when one of them remarked, "It's all African music! It's takin' over white kids' minds, turnin' 'em into monkeys, and they don't even know it!" Stunned again; stuck in deep reflection once more. What was happening? Was this all wrong?

In the dorm corridor one day, I was attracted by some very different sounds emanating from the room of a student named Dave. He was an upperclassman and not eager for my company simply on that account. But we had also had a fight once, with the end result being that I generally avoided him. But the strange music drew me like a magnet! It was jazzy, soulful, rocky, and had a choppy bounce. I peered in and soon found a place to sit amongst several other boys who were digging the sounds of Junior Walker.

The album jacket was being passed around. I held it a minute, poring over it, and thinking to myself, "I've fallen for black music!"

PART 4:   REVOLUTION

1969:

At the Academy, we were insulated from most of the ugliness going on in the world. There was one TV in my dorm, in the common room, and we had limited access to it. Whoever got to the TV set first selected what we would watch, and it was always a program of interest to teens. Nothing serious could hold our attention. Personal radio gave only smatterings of news events. Mostly all we cared about was school, acting cool, and listening to radio and records. Black music became smoother and more popular every week. Seemingly overnight, Gladys Knight, The Supremes, The Temptations, the Four Tops, and others were part of our everyday culture. Their music filled the radio waves, and for a time the only competition seemed to be hippie music.

My parents and I decided I would return to public school. It was quite a shock coming from a sophisticated, preppy environment to be infused into a county high school again. I knew about a lot of music and styles that most of the kids did not yet know. But one thing they had achieved was a far greater degree of social mutuality between whites and blacks. Black and white kids were far more social and conversant now, and most of the kids were tuned in to the current popular black music even if they would not admit it. Yet it was now less radical if anyone caught you groovin' to black music. There were more black boys on the football team, but still no black cheerleaders or black nominees for homecoming queen. However, it was heartening to see blacks meaningfully involved in 4-H. Blacks and whites still did not hang out together off-campus, or go cruising around together. But their two societies had merged far more than ever expected, and in a fairly short time.

Increasingly, TV news coverage focused on the remarkable boldness of the Civil Rights Movement. Blacks were now demanding their rights, without equivocation.

Demonstrations, mostly in the larger cities, and especially in California, were loud-and-proud, changing forever the stereotype of the complacent colored folk. They were also wanting to be called *black*, and not colored or negro. The word "black" had hitherto been considered inappropriate by both races; even embarrassing, for reasons unfathomable. But now it was the word of preference amongst our colored citizens, and whites were having to get used to the word's usage being the order of the day.

But prejudices continued. A Filipino girl transferred to our school from some state far away, and was quite a novelty. The whites did not gravitate toward her because she was "different," so she became friends with several black girls. One day she and a black girl had shared a bottle of pop, and word was buzzing among the rowdier white boys, "Did you hear? That new girl drank after a n______r !" She was shunned completely now by the white students. If there had ever been a chance for her getting to know any whites, it was completely dissolved by her drinking after a black girl.

A young white girl was overheard saying that her parents had scolded her for accepting a piece of bubble gum from a black girl on her bus, exclaiming to her, "You never take anything like that from a colored person! It could contain drugs! Don't you know that is the kind of thing they would do?"

I was walking in Rome one day and passed a fenced-in duck pond in a public park. Another white boy appeared and said, "Hey, let's climb over this fence and see if we can catch some ducks!"

I answered quietly, "Nope, better not."

"Well, I'm goin' to!"

"Better not. Besides, there comes a police car."

The boy turned toward the approaching car, then looked back at me and remarked, "He can't arrest me! He's a colored cop! They can't arrest whites!"

Maybe they could, maybe they couldn't. I ambled on my way, not caring to find out. But the fact that the boy stated it with such swift confidence gave me cause to wonder.

WHITE BOY IN THE COLORED SECTION

But black progress marched on. Soon they were on almost every variety entertainment show and even had minor scenes in other TV programs. However, black women on predominantly white shows were usually only one quarter or one eighth black, apparently to render them more conforming to a white audience. A popular musical show accepted a male black dancer as part of their regular cast. He usually performed alone. When there was a sketch or song-and-dance number requiring males and females in couples, he would remain off to one side, dancing and singing by himself. It was still taboo for him to dance with a white woman, or even sing a duet with a white man. In fact, he never got to sing except as part of a male group.

I took an after-school job bagging groceries. Black customers were frequent, but an occasional white bagger would see them coming into his line and say, "Hey, wanna trade places with me?" Some said they "didn't like waiting on coloreds," while some claimed they would not get a tip "from their kind."

I would agree to switch. I was not too proud to bag groceries for a black person. But this store also had us carry the groceries out to the customers' cars for them, and some white boys did not want to be looked upon as being in a servant role to blacks. I was proud to wait on them; I wanted to convey goodwill. Call it a sensitivity to humanity. I still identified entirely with the white world, but had a heart for all people. I could never forget the love my siblings and I had for Louise, who was no longer in our employ and thus was out of our lives. I just did not see a problem with serving a black in this capacity. Besides, they did tip me!

Everyone still said "colored people" back then. I clearly recall carting groceries out for a black woman who directed me with the words, "Just carry them over to that car, where the colored man is opening the trunk." We don't say it anymore; it was the norm back then.

I was surprised once while taking groceries to a black family's car. I recognized it as my family's former car, a 1964 Chevy wagon we had long since traded in on a new model. My first primal reaction was a feeling of superiority, in that this family rode around in a car that had already belonged to my family, when brand new. I did not think this based on their being black; I would have had the same prideful, animalistic reaction in any case. As I sat the bags into the car, I reflected a moment on all the great times my family had enjoyed in it; and now poor people owned it. Then a greater realization overcame me: I was now servant to this black family! Such a balancing of the scales; such turn-about-is-fair-play! The more I have thought about this singular event, the more I have felt a sense of balance indeed, that we both could have a sense of pride associated with that same car. It was a humbling experience, and its memory has served as a lesson in virtue that I have often shared with my own children.

One evening a black woman came through the check-out. As I bagged her groceries, I was surprised to see Old Carl behind her, obviously heavily intoxicated. They had come to Rome to shop, and apparently he was so pitifully incapacitated his wife dared not leave him at home. He was not happy if he was publicly drunk. What was happening to Old Carl? As the black world was moving upward, his was apparently drifting downward. The steady-headed Carl was not so steady after all. Beneath the solid and well-adjusted façade he had so long maintained to satisfy the expectations of the whites who ruled his world, was a crumbling soul in peril of becoming a spiritual wasteland. What could be done for Old Carl? What, indeed. I felt so sorry for his pitiable plight, I wanted to do something to bolster him. But all I could do was say "hey." At least that would give him a greater sense of social worth. So I said it. "Hey, Carl," I uttered.

Carl did not seem to hear me. His wife said, "Carl, that boy just said hey to you." He struggled to bring me into focus. I do not know if he recognized me, but he managed a faint smile and replied, "Hey dere." I could only hope Carl found strength and purpose and dignity in his life. For now, he was trying to anesthetize his entire existence.

During all the cultural upheaval being portrayed on TV, race relations continued to sail fairly smoothly at school, in our still-nascent coexistence. There were two really nice kids that got on my bus on the Kingston Highway, Sheila and Gary. They were always neatly attired and most gracious in their manner. The first time Gary and I had occasion to sit by each other on the bus, we hit it off splendidly. He was a very friendly and intelligent fellow, and we enjoyed probing each other's mind to gain cultural insights.

Gary was impressed with how much I knew about the black world. This had mostly come about by exposure to black music and studying the lives of its main artists; and particularly how black and white music had influenced each other. The more I learned about it, the more he was intrigued at my interest therein. One day he posed a question that shocked my eyes and mind wide open. He asked, "Why are you trying to be so much like black people? Most black people are trying to be like white people."

Were it not for Gary's obvious level of self-confidence and individual sense of self-worth, I might have pitied him for expressing a view that I calculated to be revelatory of his identifying with low social status. The only response I could muster was, "Naw, man! Black is where it's at these days! They got all the cool music, cool dance styles, jive talk, you name it." It was calculated to bolster his sense of equality. Some may suspect that of being an air of superiority, but I genuinely felt for his dignity.

"But you're still white. You haven't abandoned your world."

After some thought, I carefully chose my words. "Yeah, sure. It's all cool. Cool on both sides. I think we all should learn from each other, sharing the best for the best." That seemed to satisfy Gary. The conversation was sealed with his faint smile, and we did not enter into the topic again. But it seemed to present a milestone of self-discovery and social strengthening for both of us.

The term *civil rights* was in the air most of the time now. Things were moving fast. It seemed that everywhere except in Rome, Georgia, blacks were marching, protesting, even suing for their fair rights. TV shows were adding more black guests to episodes, and seemed to focus sharply on them as if to make a statement. I remember a kids' drink-mix commercial where several boys and girls were riding ponies, with the camera filming all of them at once. Then a few times the camera would abruptly zoom in closely on the one black kid, rather obviously and unnaturally, making it very clear that he was black and he was in a group of whites. I thought the gesture was well-intentioned, but at the same time phony or hypocritical. It was as though we were in Phase Two of the abrupt integration we experienced in 1966 in the schools. It wasn't happening naturally. It was so fast it seemed fake. But such is revolution.

Many school districts across the nation were being redrawn in order to infuse more blacks and whites into each other's schools, while big cities were experimenting with busing kids to other schools outside their neighborhoods in order to force integration. The day had passed when a governor with a shotgun could block black students from registering at a state's public schools or universities, and talk was going around about the Federal government planning to assess penalties to corporations and even private clubs who did not hire or admit blacks or other minorities.

Black music kept mushrooming, growing to such a dominant position that soon there was a TV show, "Soul Train," dedicated to the genre. When the white group Creedence Clearwater Revival released their song "Green River," there was such an element of Blues in it that it took root in me, and to this day remains among my top favorites. I had the unusual hope that the song would impress blacks, and black musicians in particular, as if "whites had made the grade." Talk about your complete turn-around.

I was always disturbed by news reports of racial strife, increasingly committed by blacks. Some radical white racists were blowing up black churches as if that made any sense. Yet on the local level, I never saw disharmony or disrespect between the races. People were polite, and whites where I lived, odd as it may seem, were totally averse to being rude to blacks. It was simply not done, regardless of an individual's degree of prejudice.

1970:

There is an all-black country church near Rome, on the Kingston Highway at Moran Lake Road. The members worked for many years to afford a new brick church house, but the old structure, made of aging bare wood, still stood across the road. After their services on Sundays some of the members would go over there and have a singing session in the old memory-imbued tabernacle of planks. Driving by there one Sunday, I heard them, and it was a moving and soulful sound. I drove up and parked on the roadside with my windows down, and let the stirring tones come wafting through my windows. What made their sound so different? What had they brought from Africa that blended with American hymns until it became its own art form? Why did blues and jazz and rock-n-roll evolve from it? What was its power? On occasion, following my own church services, I would take a friend or two, music aficionados, and park by the road to take in the audible feast. I loved the harmonies and heart-felt intonations, and marveled over them.

I worked for a time at the Desoto Theater in Rome. Coming off work one night, I heard black gospel singing coming from the Municipal Auditorium across Broad Street. I ventured across the way and listened on the steps a moment. Then seeing they were no longer taking tickets, I dared wander in through the lobby entrance and stood at the open doorway of the auditorium. This was a quartet of black men in blue suits. The only instrument was an electric guitar strummed by one of the singers. This being at a late point in the concert, they were really getting into it, as was their rapt audience. Except for a teenaged girl in one balcony who was doing a shimmy and waving her hands in the air, the audience were mannerly, though deeply enjoying the music.

Wearing a jacket and tie lent me some respectability, as most of the audience, all black, were dressed up. People dressed for any occasion in those days, a custom I seldom see any more, in public schools particularly. I caught the surprised look of many in attendance; I respectfully kept my distance just outside the doorway. Now I was the minority, careful not to force myself upon the scene and domain of the majority. The irony of the occasion seized me in contemplation of its novelty.

A couple of the younger ones recognized me from school, and smiled. I was hoping they would take it as a compliment that this white boy would take a look into their world. After the performance, I lingered in the lobby awhile to make sure a number of blacks saw me. I could readily discern that several of them were looking at me and then whispering words of curiosity to one another. I had created a happening; and probably another "first" for the Rome, Georgia area. Not since the night Stephen and I played with the boys in the projects had such a stark cross-racial occurrence probably taken place here. It was my way of saying I was accepting of these folks, their music, and rising culture. They didn't need it of me, but I was glad to compliment them just the same. I was careful to look all around on exiting, to see that no offended whites were watching me. There were none. This was a black event late on a dark night, and no whites but me dared invade the sanctity of it.

I was working at the Desoto one Saturday afternoon and heard a musical commotion outside. I went out to the sidewalk to determine whence it came. There was a mini-parade consisting of a single high school band, likely rented, followed by a car bearing signs to vote for—J. B. Stoner for governor! And Lester Maddox was in the back seat with him! These two men remain the largest icons of white supremacy in modern history. Oddly enough, no one seemed interested in them, beyond a brief glimpse to see what the commotion was about. They did not represent the average white Southerner, and were considered rude figures due to their bold rantings about race.

Maddox had gotten elected governor by a fluke in the election laws. No one knew at the time that Stoner was one of the infamous "church bombers." Just to be a wise-guy, I waved largely at them since no one else was doing so. They both reached out the open rear window to wave and smile very largely at me. I was the only person to wave at them, or to receive a wave in return. For a very brief moment I wondered inside if I should be more interested in their apparent stand for white Southern survival; but I knew that if white society was not to erode, it needed to avoid a deluge or even a trickle of what these two extremists offered. It was like a scene from one of Hitler's parades, yet with only one person in the street waving at these mini-Hitlers; and even then, just to be funny. I regret it to this day. They were becoming icons of a fading era, and their stars were falling. These trouble-makers were not popular. *Already the race revolution was afoot.*

Black students were being given opportunities to participate in talent demonstrations during school assemblies in the gym. Some sang songs or performed personal skills during the entertainment segment. George had a unique talent, and was offered the showcase to present it. He worked at a large shoe repair shop in Rome, Georgia, running its shoe-shine stand. He was amazing at making his rag pop while making dance steps in place. His "performance" would attract passersby and bring in more business from the street. Perhaps one of the most astounding displays of irony came the day the principal signed George up to provide his style of showmanship: popping his shoe-shine rag loudly and rhythmically while dancing around on the gym floor in boogie fashion. The students and faculty loved it. I glanced around at some black students and noticed some were smiling, one was laughing, but most sat in silence. What could have been viewed as stereotyping, or presenting George as a demeaning caricature, was actually an honor in its own way. It was what George could do, and owing to his never ending showmanship, there was nothing he would rather do. By the time he was finished, most of the black students seemed to approve, deeming his act a milestone of social progress in its own unique and ironic way.

As soon as high school was out, I enlisted in the Army at age seventeen. At the induction center in Atlanta, one could readily discern the whites who avoided blacks entirely. They were usually low-bred and unrefined. Likewise, a few blacks gravitated to the opposite end of the barracks, uncomfortable with mixing with whites at this early juncture. Otherwise, whites and blacks were fairly courteous to one another. We were there for three days, undergoing physical exams and batteries of written tests. A young black recruit bunked below me. He was so poor, there were holes in his clothes, even his underwear, but he was the most cheerful and friendly of young men. We got to joking around and talking about our home towns, favorite activities, etc. He seemed incapable of incurring the wrath of anyone, even the most racial of whites. I was deeply impressed by his virtuous ways, and broad acceptance of all of God's creatures, regardless of color. I lay atop my bunk thinking about what all he may have gone through, growing up. I could only assume that with good parenting and solid faith, he had developed into an upright and outstanding character. Though poor temporally, he was rich in spirit. I was certain he would go on to exert a very favorable influence upon the white world he was about to encounter, despite the limited opportunities for his race.

I was very cordial with that poor fellow. In my heart I wanted him to feel good about himself. It was sort of like a mental mission I was now finding myself on, quick to show courtesy to blacks and other minorities, hoping to instill within them a ray of pride. It may sound like a superior attitude now, but in my juvenile mind it was meant as pure virtue. They did not need a "white knight" to rescue them; but I could not resist the endeavor, ever so subtle, of sowing goodwill.

A throng of us white and black soldiers rode a bus from Atlanta to Fort Jackson, South Carolina, for basic training. We were tired and it grew dark, so there was little interaction. Once we got underway with the boot camp routine, I was surprised at how many black drill sergeants we had, as well as a Mexican. There were several Puerto Rican trainees in my company as well. I did not realize they were American citizens, and thus subject to the draft. I was later to learn that many blacks and Puerto Ricans stayed in the Army for a stable career.

A black NCO, Staff Sergeant Stribling, was my platoon's drill sergeant. He was all business, and when he said jump, we flew. Not since Louise and her switch had a black person had the slightest degree of authority over me. Sgt. Stribling was such a tough soldier, he made me wish I was back under the auspices of Louise. The Alabama recruit who bunked under me was a walking time-bomb of rage, a wiry yet tough redneck of the strictest order. He was not a fair representative of the good majority of people in Alabama, yet ironically was among those racial extremists causing all Alabamans to be cast as bigots. One day we came in from training and he spouted off to me, "Well, how do ya like havin' a n_______r tellin' ya what to do!"

I had never had occasion to answer such a question, and had no rejoinder handy. I casually replied, "Well, I had a colored maid as a kid, and she had authority to tell us what to do. I guess it doesn't bother me as much..."

His glare gave me the impression that I had already said too much. His goggle-like glasses magnified his searing eyes, and I thought for a moment that laser beams would emanate from them, and burn holes through me. Suddenly he seemed to hate me as much as he hated blacks. He never spoke to me again, and avoided me at every turn.

During pugil stick training, (mock bayonet fighting with helmets and padded sticks,) he came at me with full fury. He looked like he would enjoy killing me, even if only for pretend during training exercises. I immediately sensed the need to defend myself rigorously from this wild boy, who despised me for nothing more than having a benign attitude toward blacks. I battled away at him, but slipped in the wood shavings and fell on my back. He was trying to "stab" me, thrusting downward with the tip of his stick, which would give him a win; but I had a never-say-die spirit. I kicked and swatted his pugil stick away until I was able to regain my feet, and give him a sound thrashing. When Sgt. Stribling saw I was getting the better of him, he blew his whistle, ending the bout. This black NCO who was the object of Bama Boy's ire indeed had authority: the authority to save a hater of blacks from a brutal beating, by one who leaned toward their dignity.

There was a very amiable black trainee in my company, one of those good-old-country boys you just like to chat and hang out with. He was so humble and polite, and had interesting tales about country life. He was the personable type who soon get called by their first name rather than by last; soldiers call each other by the last name unless they become close friends. But soon fellows were calling him by his given name, which was Ethel. It was pronounced EE-thul, and not the obvious feminine form. So countrified was he, that his parents had not realized his name would one day be confused with a girl name. No one made fun of his name, either. Not that he was a bully. He was on the contrary a gentle soul, although big and strong enough to take care of himself. He was respected because he was so good-natured, and because most whites really did not want to make fun of a black. So he would patiently explain that his name was EE-thul, and not Ethel, and people accepted that.

Bama Boy would grimace whenever he saw me speaking with Ethel, and shake with rage if we joked around, helped each other with our equipment, or took photos of each other to send to the folks back home. Bama Boy was stressed most of each training day, whenever Sgt. Stribling was ordering us around. I channeled my energies into my training performance, and could not have cared less that our drill sergeant was black. Yet up to that point Stribling's towering over me with complete control was one of the hugest novelties of my life. My parents and grandparents would never have dreamed that day would ever come.

Blacks did not hold back in hand-to-hand combat training. They were in it like all the others: to do their best, to stand tall, and be a man. There was no hate or excessive aggression in it, just a confident full-on involvement. It was nevertheless an unprecedented spectacle to behold. I was still balancing the Mr. Hyde element of resenting blacks being aggressive toward whites, with the opposing view from my mental mission of wishing them well. It takes a lot of time and hard, intentional effort to weed out racism; and like weeds, it will grow back if not carefully watched. *Sometimes culture must be cultivated.*

My Grandpa Turner was in the Army in World War I, and related to me how the Army was officially segregated back then. He said they never served together. I asked, "Didn't you at least see any black troops in the war?"

Grandpa replied, "Yeah, but they'd be a ways off, and headed someplace else. And if they came near our area, the white soldiers would look off and walk a different way if they saw a black officer coming, so they wouldn't have to salute him."

There were so many Puerto Ricans in my company, I began to hang out with some of them, in order to learn something of their language and culture. I had an interest in foreign languages, although to date my only coursework had been in Latin. I had never been around Hispanics growing up. Although I was reasonably educated and cultured, I simply knew nothing about them; they did not live all over the nation as they now do. Thus my fascination with my first exposure to what I considered "foreigners" gained impetus from the rarity of it all.

As illogic would have it, or the irony of racist logic, there were some white trainees who shunned me for associating with the Puerto Ricans. Some even criticized me for it. These were not just Southern whites, either, but from all over. Only my more cultured or at least good-natured associates were cool with it. One of the most critical was from the upper Midwest, and one from the extreme Northeast. I doubted most of these whites had been around Hispanics any more than I had, but somehow they had picked up an unexpected loathing and aversion to them. There was just a natural disdain for these fellows based on apparently nothing. I rather liked them; they were for the most part cheery and friendly, and were willing to teach me some Spanish.

Some of the boys in the barracks would tell rude Puerto Rican jokes, those from large cities where they had learned such derogatory humor. Some of us smaller-town guys would just sit and wonder how all that animosity and racial disrespect came about in the first place. I could see no basis for it. Most of us knew nothing of Hispanics, so were confused over how a universal rejection could have been generated for them or any ethnic group, while not assessing each individual for his own worth or character. Again, overt prejudice seemed to originate mainly from the less refined of society, the bully boys who were both tasteless and devoid of much virtue. And perhaps those who needed to look down on someone else in order to feel better about themselves.

Through training and on into regular service in the Army, I grew very accustomed to blacks and Puerto Ricans, and indeed people from many nationalities and ethnic backgrounds. I thought less and less about race, especially when sharing living quarters, showers, mess halls, and job duties. If there was a guitar around, I played a lot of blues, which seemed to impress and please many of the blacks. I learned a couple of Spanish tunes as well, gaining me friendship with Hispanics. It was a nice feeling: bridging all differences of background with the universal language of music.

The Army was another great leveling ground, much like high school football had been, wherein was found a natural catalyst for melding uncommon elements: a focus on duty and the absolute need for teamwork, even when forced as it was. I never knew what happened to Bama Boy after boot camp. I can only imagine he had a series of uphill struggles ahead of him, in the societal sense. I imagine at some juncture the Army forced him to attend one of their newly-formed Race Relations classes, though he would probably have gone AWOL before attending!

1971:

Vietnam brought a stark contrast to my months of training. Simply put, whites and blacks in combat together tended to form a mutual respect and comradery. But those on the ghetto-like bases tended to polarize. I witnessed a great deal of hostility on the part of many black troops in the garrison camps. Blacks tended to remain distant and aloof. They even had a manual communication modality called "dapping," which I never comprehended, but which was instinctively understood by them. Blacks would approach each other, and even if they had never met before, would silently go into a routine of different hand gestures including patting, slapping, rapping, gripping, and symbols made with joined grips. They really put a rhythm to it, and it was entertaining to watch. Just like whites, blacks grew closer and more introverted and hostile, as a means of survival. Whites were not as defensively united as a race, but whether individually or collectively, likewise developed a withdrawn toughness as a means of coping.

Too, in the mainstream Army there were blacks from many backgrounds, including those from inner-city ganglands and places where liberation protests were the order of the day. True, many of these were around in basic training, but their full personalities and inclinations were not allowed room for expression under the austerity of boot camp. But here in the real-life Army a microcosm of racial America had developed, with all its stressors being magnified. As a natural consequence, occasional hotspots erupted in the form of rebellion and violence. What perhaps saved the garrison camps from riots and constant violence was the sad fact that a surprising number of troops, black, white, and otherwise, were deactivating themselves when off-duty, with intake of various intoxicants. Various enclaves retreated from reality. It was survival by withdrawal.

There was also racial discrimination amongst the US troops, toward the native Vietnamese. Coming into the country we were issued some pamphlets to explain local dangers, as well as customs. I do not recall seeing anyone else reading them, but I studied avidly the Vietnamese cultural mores and customs. I wanted to respect them in their own country, being naïve to the massive hostility the GI's held for the natives. It did not take long for me to size up the situation: the natives were not popular with most Americans. This was largely due to us suffering so far from home without support from our nation, nor much apparent appreciation from the natives. But of course there was a major race factor at play as well. Throughout my tour many GI's of all races spoke derisively of them, and often insulted them. Sometimes they were brutalized.

I was also sensitive to certain gestures that offended them, such as waving, calling someone over by curling the finger, talking to them with hands on hips, or letting them see the bottom of the foot. These and many other acts were strictly taboo in their culture. If I admonished a GI to avoid certain expressions or gestures, some would thank me, while others would grumble racial epithets against the people. "I'll act any way I want to! I'm an American! I'm not from here!" was an often-heard reaction.

But many Vietnamese also expressed discrimination against us. It was offensive to most of them if a GI married a Vietnamese. A GI entering a village or street or place of business where Americans were seldom or never seen, resulted in shocked looks from the locals. Nevertheless, the Vietnamese laborers and troops were generally very friendly with us. Overall, it seemed that they, too, had the same general distribution of racism throughout their society as did we, furthering my conclusion that universally the human constitution is based significantly upon racial preference and exclusion.

Over time I came to resent any Vietnamese who was not polite to us, deducing that if they did not appreciate all we are sacrificing for them, they were no better than enemy. I did react gruffly to some of them on occasion, but for the most part I went out of my way to ingratiate myself to them, hoping it would help cement their allegiance to us.

The racial progress between blacks and whites I thought I had witnessed in basic and advanced training seemed to have evaporated in the 'Nam. My first day there, I saw a white soldier walk past a group of five blacks.

He turned and growled at one of them, "What're you smiling at?"

One of the blacks turned and replied, "Huh? What you talking about?"

"You think something's cute? What was the wise-guy grin all about?"

The two began to grapple. I sat atop a bunker with a friend, watching the scene unfold. Soon two other blacks came over and held the white soldier while the insulted one punched him with ease. But he was wily and slipped loose. He stormed away in a rage, yelling, "You boys can't fight one at a time, can ya?"

I had heard that expression before, and considered it a stereotypical concept based in racism, but I saw before my very eyes three blacks roughing up a single white. He may have had it coming, but it would have been better form for only the one offended black to fight him, I figured. Being torn between the white soldier provoking it, and the black soldiers outmanning him, it was difficult to take sides. Besides, it was over so fast, I just sat and marveled over it awhile. But for the first time in my life, I saw blacks taking a violent stand, and there was no turning back. The gate containing deep-rooted resentment was flung open, and anything was possible now.

Most every time I saw blacks passing near each other, they would share a silent "Black Power" sign with raised fists. I saw one black troop with the brim of his boonie hat embroidered in black thread, "All Power To The Black People." Now this alarmed me, even insulted me. I wondered in my teenaged mind if it were really coming to this: black people taking over, violently and completely, as some were now expressing as a desired goal.

A white soldier I knew of had somehow offended a black soldier in camp, and one night while walking to his hut was confronted by him, and half a dozen others. They surrounded him, some pulling out knives. He narrowly escaped what seemed a deadly fate. White racist extremists had done the same thing to blacks in the past, but due to successes by the Civil Rights Movement, most of that had ceased. And constituents of the redneck factor in the 'Nam were usually too boozed up to care anymore. But these were not the blacks I had gone to school with. Not all black troops ganged up like that, but some formerly passive ones did gravitate to the power-center of this new form of black solidarity.

Were it not for seeing better harmony between the races when out in the killing fields, I might have built a very high wall of separation between myself and blacks whenever I was back on post. They didn't need Whitey, didn't want him, and were busy building their own social fortress. What more did they want? At least in the Army, they had many positions of power and authority now. Whites were correcting each other when one made a racist remark. Whites were disdaining racist expression amongst their own, and seemed to be more willing to accept blacks at this crucial juncture in the evolution of American society than vice versa. But many blacks were seizing the opportunity to break out more fully and completely than ever before, like magma spewing through cracks in the rocky crust of oppression that had held them down for centuries. It was bound to happen, and it was happening now.

After several months in 'Nam, I was growing callous and bordering on pitiless. I longed for a sense of dignity and humanity which seemed to have been taken away by service in this land of living nightmares. I received an unexpected spiritual boost and a renewal of faith in life in the form of a wounded enemy. As combat medics, we served Americans first, allies second, and wounded enemy last—unless triage indicated one of the second or third group required more prompt and serious treatment. We were working on saving a wounded Viet Cong guerilla when he began to mumble some words in Vietnamese, "Nuoc. Toi muon nuoc. Nuoc." Usually an interrogator and interpreter from Intel or the CIA would be present to question them, as they came fresh from battle, with the battle sometimes still in progress.

"I wonder what he's saying," the others uttered.

I knew just enough basic words and phrases to assist me in wartime duties. "He's asking for water," I answered. I fetched some water and held his head as he drank from it. Despite his agony, he was able to make a faint smile of gratitude. At this very moment I felt a spiritual presence reminding me of the Scripture, *"If your enemy thirsts, give him to drink."*

Within that brief but shining moment, I felt a surge of hope and life-purpose welling up in me. I felt somehow safe from the flames of hell lapping away at us. I thought upon this singular episode for some time, and began to realize therefrom that I could overcome all biases and hatred toward any group of people. Though my hatred for the evil VC was a natural result of war, the capacity to despise others—whether races or creeds or political parties—even Communists—could be extricated from within me, and I did not have to hate in order to function. How I came to long for all peoples to have the blessing of that insight.

1972:

After enduring the sadness of Vietnam, and miraculously escaping with my life, I was thrilled beyond measure to finally receive orders to return home. Returning black and white soldiers were equally happy, sharing in their mutual mirth while processing out, and preparing to board what we called the Freedom Bird to fly back to the country which had sent us to hell. We hoped we were going to Heaven. I had no idea what to expect racially or socially, back home. I had heard about race riots, but they were being downplayed now by anti-war turbulence. I was certain that social advances had been made by minorities, as I had seen in the Army.

After a month of leave time with my family, I was ready to drive the five hours to Fort Gordon in Augusta, which was my new duty station. Having served as a combat medic, I was now assigned to work my final year as a medic in Army psychiatry. Most of the patients were young and had suffered complete and total breakdowns. There were about as many blacks and Puerto Ricans as there were white patients. Severity of cases ranged from moderate to extreme. Some were able to return to duty, while some were medically discharged.

Many of the black patients also carried a deep hostility and refused to cooperate with white staff. Black staff would often be assigned to their care. Several Puerto Ricans expressed hostility at having been drafted, and protested their homeland being a US territory. None of the Puerto Ricans I served with expressed that sentiment, but the stressed-out inpatients certainly dwelt upon it. Many of them exhibited similar symptoms and behaviors, which the staff referred to as the "Puerto Rican Syndrome." This was manifested by a number of factors, chiefly claiming to have seen either a vision of Mother Mary, or of their own mother, peering in the window at them and expressing disdain over their illness, as if the patients themselves had failed in life. They would often go smash out a window pane with their bare fist, and end up being held down by a mob of white-uniformed staff while getting a shot of Thorazine, followed by stitches in the hand and temporary confinement in a seclusion cell.

Most of these patients were coming from Germany, Korea, and Vietnam, where sociological norms were confusing, securities of home were lost, and drugs were rampantly available. White and black cases ran the full spectrum of diagnoses, with the only repeated pattern being the racial hostility held by many blacks. I found that if I could win the trust of the agitated black patients, to the point that we could speak openly without the walls of race between us, we could reach some common core within us, thereby enabling not only the patient to come to a higher degree of emotional comfort, but enhancing my sense of mutual humanity as well.

I had black pals working in the ward and living in my barracks. These were young soldiers barely out of training, who had never been to Vietnam. Black Vietnam veterans carried a double load of resentment. Most 'Nam vets were burdened by mistreatment by our country during the war and after coming home. Black troops bore that burden, while also perceiving it as an added dimension of the white world which had thrust them into it in the first place. But the guys in the barracks were just the regular old fellers I was accustomed to back home. It was very impressive to me that I could form very relaxed friendships with blacks from many backgrounds, even stereotypically hardcore hotbeds of racial strife like New York and Chicago. Friendship is always possible; it is not just about race.

1973:

I was winding up my last year in the Army. Working in the hospital at Fort Gordon, one day a black mental patient escaped the ward. He was yelling in the street about wanting to kill all the whites in the whole Army. Being the senior medic on duty, I went outside and told him to come back in. He refused. I was soon surrounded by white medics, young and untested, who stood gawking. I ordered one of them to go call the military police, but he just stood there. None of them would obey my repeated order. Then I said, "We have to take him. Somebody get a nurse to prepare an injection." Then turning to the patient again, I explained, "You need to come inside. Regulations. If not, we'll have to escort you inside."

The patient was storming around wildly, then came charging at me with full fury. I ordered the boys to help me subdue him, but they stood frozen to the ground. It wasn't just their lack of experience, it was chiefly the likelihood that none had ever shown assertiveness toward a black, and being so averse to it, were not about to start now. How the tables had turned! The white population had by this time in history been so groomed toward nonaggressiveness toward the blacks, who had suffered at the hands of the less scrupulous whites for so long, that it was unthinkable for most whites to even think of holding forth against a black.

The patient now attacked me, and I fended him off with defensive punches and near-kicks. I kept him at bay long enough to go inside and try to call the MP's and summon an injection. By the time I reached the desk, the patient had run back into the ward, and was coming at me full stream. He had brought a mop from the rack outside, broken its head off, and was about to attack me with it. I yanked open the utility closet and grabbed a broom, and we clashed as if in pugil stick training. Soon a male nurse, a lieutenant, rushed onto the scene and ordered the staff to subdue the patient. Older medics on the scene took to the task, indicative of much more experience, while the younger ones were slow to action. A couple of them finally joined in, but in his wild thrashing, eased their grip on him a moment and he got back to his feet. He and I threw some punches until they could tackle him back down again. Soon the nurse had injected him in the hip with Thorazine, which rapidly eased him to sleep.

The patient awoke in a seclusion cell, strapped to his bed. As it happened, he was neither psychotic nor neurotic, but suffered from a character-behavioral disorder. As such, he was deemed responsible for his actions, and was transferred to the post stockade under guard by the MP's. I was ordered to the Judge Advocate General's office to provide a statement regarding the event. I asked the lawyer in charge of the case if the man could be released from prison and placed under close psychiatric care, including medication to calm his hostility. The lawyer said the only way I could get him out of jail was to make a statement to the effect that the clash had been my own fault. I regretfully shook my head and replied, "No, sir. He's the culprit. I suppose he's to remain in the stockade. But for how long?"

"May not be too long," the lawyer-captain replied. Depends on whether they court-martial him or give him company-level punishment."

Without my knowledge, he was released in two weeks. Due to a long series of behavior problems in the Army, he was being discharged. Luckily I was out of town visiting my folks when he and two other black soldiers came to my barracks looking for me one night. Before he left the Army, he aimed to "make me pay." My black barracks friends told me about it, and how he was planning to attack me in my sleep. They had told him I would not be back for a good while—not sure when—likely causing him and his little gang to give up on trying to get revenge on me. Race may have partially encouraged his rage, but my black friends, everyday sorts, were loyal to me and to the cause of decency. I emerged from the experience not negatively influenced by race, but by a further realization that the average black fellow was an okay guy.

Black Power was the most dominant theme in the air by this time. Blacks were getting loud and proud, and letting everyone know that Civil Rights were now in style. It was in music, movies, posters, clothing fads, and jive slang. Affirmative Action was gaining strength and white violence against blacks was almost a thing of the past. Discrimination still happened, but was by now so taboo, that white businesses and institutions were generally going to great effort to avoid any hint of it. And the City Pool in Rome, Georgia, formerly for whites only, was now all black.

1974:

After the Army and prior to college, I worked in Atlanta for a year. I found decent lodging in an elderly lady's boarding house in Brookhaven. She had never had a man in the building before, just elderly ladies, and would introduce me to any guests who came to see her, as she thought I made a favorable impression on them. She wanted them to know that the man in her house was a gentleman.

One such acquaintance of hers, an author, was staying with her a few days. She was writing a book about Dr. Martin Luther King's family; and though she was white, had been invited by his kindly parents to sit with them in the fabled Ebenezer Church on the approaching Sunday. This was a prized prospect for anyone, let alone a white woman. She was proud to have the opportunity.

Due to a number of factors, she was unable to arrive in time, and missed this golden adventure. But a fate worse than this narrowly missed her: A deranged young black man had burst into the service with two pistols and began shooting wildly. One bullet struck Mrs. King, sadly resulting in her death. Another parishioner was also killed.

Later I saw the visitor in the foyer of the house, and asked how her visit and interview with the Kings had gone.

She was pale and looked a bit faint. She recounted to me the day's tragic events. I had to sit on the porch a moment and reflect on this upsetting news. Deep in my mind I was glad the assailant was a black man, for if a white had done it, Atlanta would have erupted into civil war.

But when the news first hit the streets, the average black citizen did not know it was committed by a black. An uprising was beginning to stir when Mayor Jackson, the first black mayor of any major US city, appealed to the public to remain calm. So tense was the issue of racial inequality, that events smaller than this could easily ignite unrest in the streets. The progress I had seen in race relations was not yet so uniform as I had supposed. At my job there was ideal harmony between white and black employees. However, down on the mean streets of day-to-day urban survival, things were still edgy. I was often warned by whites to stay out of south Atlanta, where whites were routinely targeted by black criminals and racists alike.

I was riding a motorcycle in those days, (an act of foolishness which thankfully I've convinced my children to avoid at all costs.) The night Hank Aaron of the Braves was expected to hit his record-breaking home run, I drove to the Atlanta Stadium so I could say I had been there when it happened. Having never been to the stadium, I was surprised when the exit ramp off the freeway degraded into a narrow dark street which cut through the midst of an impoverished black neighborhood.

I couldn't drive very far, as the street was packed with partying folks, madly celebrating this tremendous event in black history. It was a moment of glory for them, and although I was a Hank Aaron fan, to see these ardent revelers suggested that this was exclusively their day. And I was on their turf.

I tried to inch along, and the crowd just turned and grinned at me. They were not moving aside. Many were eying me over as if I were a target for their frustrations. Some looked amused at the oddity of my presence, while some appeared angry that I would dare invade this, their moment of glory. I kept smiling and nodding as I moved at a snail's pace through the mob. Slowly, ever slowly, they would finally drift out of my path and allow me to advance through this massive sea of human flesh. Then the crowd would again envelop around me, until I was enclosed within their assemblage, and at their mercy.

Some of them were pretty high and itching for some kind of action. I prayed and tried to breathe steadily as I expected a knife to enter my ribs at any moment. But bless those people's hearts, they finally let me through, and I drove up to the edge of the stadium right when "it" happened! The stadium exploded into riotous cheering, which lasted for a goodly amount of time, assuring me that Hank had just made his historic mark in baseball—and in my little way I was there to witness it. Not since my war days had I seen history being made before my eyes, and it was a thrill indeed.

I explored around and found a different route home! But I hoped those black baseball fans had appreciated my courteous smiling and slow, respectful speed as I invaded their very special happening. I was convinced that there was still much to accomplish between our races, despite advances made to date.

1980's – 1990's:

These two decades are a blur of memories, so much was happening in the world at large, and within my narrow segment of it. Career, family, home owning, all kept me too busy to worry about world affairs. But black progress marched on. The Civil Rights movement did not lose a step in its determined pace.

I did have to go into some black parts of cities on business, particularly in Savannah and Atlanta, and did not sense anxiety over my safety unless I had read the crime reports in the papers, and became aware of the inherent risks of entering certain areas. Besides, there are plenty of dangerous white neighborhoods, I am sure. But being made aware of the hot danger zones of these cities, I always traveled armed, being reflexively reminded of the tense dangers lurking back in old Saigon. This meant keeping my suit coat on in the hottest of weather, to conceal my 9mm. I am glad I never had to use it. I am sure my faith in God, and avoidance of the meanest sections of town, shielded me significantly.

I was saddened to see for the first time in any city, bars over the doors and windows of doctors' offices in all-black communities. Rather than just walk in, one had to push a button and wait to be buzzed in. On average I am sure most whites still lived better than most blacks, but for the life of me I was always astounded at how this race barrier could linger on. Blacks in the ghettos were simply not advancing. Abhorrence of anything white remained the order of the day. Despite historic advances in freedom and equality and opportunities, in a way it appeared black hatred of the white world was worse than it had ever been. It continued to reinforce itself and resultantly it was very dangerous for whites to venture onto their turf.

The enslaving nature of government social handouts seemed to keep these unfortunate ones ensnared within a no-exit societal conundrum. Then along came a new form of slavery: rap music. It seems to enslave the mind, with its driving, never-changing tempo and hideous language and themes. Music videos, black or white, were immoral and demoralizing in the extreme, but rap "music" seemed to seal people's minds and souls into non-thinking robotic carelessness. I hoped against hope that moving ahead with dignity and equality for blacks would magnify their good and decent majority.

1992:

The racial revolution keeps revolving: I pulled into a small Georgia city on some business. Police were barricading a main street leading to the downtown square. I inquired as to what was taking place. An officer informed me that on this particular Saturday of each year, the Ku Klux Klan held a rally and parade! I was stunned, thinking this was pretty much a part of the past. Disbelief, as much as curiosity, compelled me to walk up to the barricade, where I was further astonished to see some 150 policemen in full riot gear, including city police, county deputies, and state troopers. One group of them were lined up in two ranks, the front row down on one knee, reminiscent of

Revolutionary War scenes. What was going to happen? I thought it was the end of the world.

Soon I could hear a man somewhere on a public address system shouting out a speech about white power. His words reached a fever pitch before he was done. Then came the parade; or lack thereof. Perhaps a half dozen Klansmen marched up the street, clad in their robes and caps. That was it. About as many skinheads walked with them, voicing racial slurs against the one black woman who stood to watch. I expected something drastic to happen; it never did. It was over in a few moments, and I almost chuckled at the tremendous display of security forces for the little demonstration that seemed to have no impact because it no longer had wind in its sails. Long gone were the days when Klan rallies could draw 10,000 to 20,000, many of them doctors, lawyers, professors, and other prominent white citizens. Now this little anachronism from a bygone era, too, was obviously gone with the wind.

2000's:

The Confederate battle flag was removed from the Georgia state flag. This was a natural consequence of blacks, and some whites, suggesting racism inherent in the flag. There was considerable outcry from many white Georgians that the flag represented part of our heritage and was an honor to the struggles and suffering of our Confederate ancestors. And of course, this flag was only adopted by the state in 1956, reputedly as a staunch stand against blacks by the legislature. No matter—if there is a minority outcry in America today, the minority eventually wins out. It was probably a good thing, though: the Confederate battle flag has fallen from its former battle glory, and been adopted by white supremacists who wave it as a constant reminder of their hatred for blacks. I always said it did not represent race to me, but history; yet deep inside I was reluctant to display it if blacks were around. Semi-consciously I felt it was surely overbearing racially. Such has been the conflict of my life, sorting, analyzing, and starting all over again.

It proved of no real consequence that a few blacks fought for the South, and some of their descendants proudly claim membership in the Sons of Confederate Veterans. After a long fight from grassroots level up to the legislature, a compromise was reached by issuing a new flag with a gold seal in the center, bordered by little flags that formerly flew over Georgia since pre-colonial times, down through the Confederate era. It was considered by an international flag club to be the ugliest banner of its day. It looked acceptable on paper, but in reality it just wouldn't "fly."

Due to popular rejection of the new state flag, another compromise was reached by returning to the original state seal on three broad stripes of red, white, and blue, representing the original formal Confederate national flag. Nothing racist can be seen in it. But also "gone with the wind" are the genuine blood-stained Confederate battle flags which once hung on display in the capitol building, outside the governor's office. The song "Dixie" is practically *verboten*, and will likely never be heard in public again. I mention the foregoing because they were real events in my life which completely turned my world around. For the most part there have been many good changes, especially those which have wrought more fairness for blacks. I still like the tune "Dixie;" Lincoln liked it. To me, Dixieland is not a prejudice, it is just a place.

In 2015 the State of Georgia announced that, as of 2016, the two remaining Confederacy-oriented government employee holidays, Robert E. Lee's Birthday and Confederate Memorial Day, would both simply be renamed "State Holiday." These two lasted twenty-one years after Jefferson Davis' Birthday was dropped as a state employees' holiday, and twenty-nine years after MLK Day was adopted.

Some states' governments did not drop holidays for Confederate heroes' birthdays, but joined their names with King's:

In Alabama, Martin Luther King, Jr. Day is known as "Robert E. Lee—Martin Luther King Birthday".

WHITE BOY IN THE COLORED SECTION

In Arkansas, Martin Luther King, Jr. Day is known as "Dr. Martin Luther King Jr. and Robert E. Lee's Birthdays".

In Mississippi, Martin Luther King, Jr. Day is known as "Martin Luther King's and Robert E. Lee's Birthdays".

In Virginia, it was known as Lee–Jackson–King Day, combining King's birthday with the established Lee–Jackson Day. In 2000, Lee–Jackson Day was moved to the Friday before Martin Luther King Jr. Day, establishing Martin Luther King Jr. Day as a holiday in its own right.

Today, it is impossible to find an American city of any size, that does not have a street named after Dr. King.

Perhaps it was no coincidence that I just happened to stumble across two amazingly racial movies at the time of this writing, which caused me to reflect sharply upon where we all came from, and where we have arrived. One is called "The Sun Shines Bright," (1953), which is a sequel to "Judge Priest" (1937.) In both films, situated in the Post-Civil War era of the South, all the blacks are caricatured as ignorant, cowering, comical figures guided along by benevolent whites who control all facets of society. "Judge Priest" is mostly comical. "The Sun Shines Bright" is semi-comical, but culminates in a white mob wanting to lynch an innocent young black man. The victim is saved by a white leader of the community, the benevolent neo-Massa of the town. In both films, the white leader gets mobs to calm down by arranging for blacks to play "Dixie," restoring a sense of "decency and stability."

At the same time I discovered, ironically, a 1962 film called "The Intruder." This film was so shocking and stark in dealing with racial issues, it pretty much died on the vine and was never famous. White society was not ready for it. It starred a young William Shatner as a self-proclaimed "social reformer," come to stir up white supremacist sentiment in a little town on the dawn of integration of the local school. I have mentioned how "racially sanitized" movies and indeed all of American society was in those days: no emphasis on blacks, whether favorable or not; and especially no use of the "N-word."

How stunned I was to hear Shatner yelling out the "N-word" all through the film. He gets the town so upset, they are ready to block integration by force. He manages to get a black youth accused of a heinous crime which never even happened, and just before he is lynched, a benevolent white man breaks up the mob and exposes the "reformer" for the fraud he is.

In both the 1953 and 1962 films, "white authority," or strong white leadership presence, defuse the mobs. Racially dominant as this may seem, it was likely necessary to "protect" real-life black communities from white wrath. If a black authority figure had featured prominently in either film, seeds of social discord would have been sown.

The primary difference in the old films and the newer one is, that in the latter the blacks were portrayed as decent, intelligent, peaceful people who just wanted to go to school. Though one sees a major white slant in the films, at least the latter one, despite its shocking and frequent dropping of the "N-bomb," was actually an attempt to garner some equality for blacks in the eyes of the viewing audience. But by its very nature, it was doomed to fail financially and publicly, owing to its release during the controversial situation of the year 1962. Reportedly, the people of the town where it was filmed protested it being filmed there; "it simply was not done."

If I ever had occasion to doubt the inspiration of writing the accounts contained within this book, seeing these films just as I neared its completion reassured me that this book was meant to come forth. Consider the parallels.

PART 5: DEVOLUTION

Devolution, in the sense of downward progression, seems to have displaced much of the race-relations progress our society has made heretofore. That is, if one believes the news broadcasts, or listens to agitators. It is an act of evil to suggest that all blacks are being constantly tormented by all whites in this day and age. I think people in the slums, *of any race*, have a self-esteem problem which they learned from their environment, and attempt to deal with it by slamming other races. This is pitiful, especially in the face of how far most whites have gone to make amends for their white ancestors.

Just when I was thinking that today's urban blacks-against-police problem was generally unjustified, along comes a case where some white cops may have been proven prejudiced. If so, that will come to light and be legally corrected. But for the most part, it seems that the larger portion of these problems is being agitated by a relatively slim minority of urban dwellers and we need to give justice a chance.

Before their passing, former governors and avowed segregationists George Wallace and Lester Maddox made public apology for their discriminatory efforts earlier in their careers, and indeed were documented for their many generous acts to the benefit of blacks and other minorities. Many former white racists grew softer in their hearts, and the white race in general began policing one another carefully to avoid any unkind word or deed toward minorities. Racist jokes, among whites, have become taboo and are eschewed except by the least refined.

However, much of this progress has been undone by agitators who never seem satisfied that blacks have achieved pretty much everything they set out to gain. Whites and blacks enjoy the best social relationships in history, yet there are still pockets of racism in the ghettos continually stirred up by agitators, usually political figures who seem to gain something by "playing the race card" at every turn. It echoes the words of my Mom, that paranoia can easily enter into race relations.

My Mom, a psychiatric nurse, once told me, "One must be gentle with blacks, because all blacks are paranoid."

"Isn't that a rather general statement?" I asked, surprised.

"It is very hard to find one who is not. And it's not their fault. They were set up for it by white society."

I do know that many whom I meet even today are very sensitive to the topic of race. Despite all our progress, I cannot speak of race-related topics with most blacks, who express a sensitivity that makes me wince. Even if I have something positive to say, such as commenting on how black music has transformed the world, or how great the contributions of MLK were, the mere mention of race seems to stir up discomfort. I am grateful for close black friends who nevertheless encouraged my writing of this book.

Many counterproductive race-based traditions linger on in the 21st Century. Perhaps they always will. There have been times when I was having difficulty locating the home of a black person, and their neighbors would not give me directions. They would usually reply with something on the line of "Seems like he lived around here a long time ago," or "He moved away," only to finally find after much effort the person lived next door or across the hall. I was never offended by this. A white man showing up in a suit asking for the whereabouts of a black man traditionally spelled danger, and I would take it as a matter of course. I adapted by making absolutely sure of the address and how to find it, then walking briskly in and out, to minimize concern among the neighbors. I wised up with time to have black clients meet me at a restaurant, treat on me. It worked out best all round that way.

High crime continues to exist in predominantly black neighborhoods; black-on-black crime, ironically. In neighborhoods where whites are not welcome, it seems blacks suffer the most crime against one another. Whenever I would do business on the south side of Atlanta, I carried my gun permit and a 9mm 18-round pistol under my suit coat. I never had to use it, but south Atlanta was and still is the scene of daily murders. I asked a black friend from that area what it was like growing up in south Atlanta. He replied, "Oh, it used to be nice. We only had one murder a week. Nowadays, there is one every day!"

It is pleasing to see the great advances blacks have made in all fields of endeavor. As the old saying goes, "You've come a long way, baby." Those blacks who find a way out of the ghetto tend to find a better life. But it would be racist to suggest that they all disband their assemblage of fellow blacks in order to extricate themselves from the slum life. Those who do make it big leave the slums, and do not remain as local role models. Too often the only local role models are pushers, in their big fine cars, inspiring many youths to a life of crime. Still, some of the most sterling characters in America or any nation are those who, despite growing up in a ghetto, live up to positive principles of honor instilled in them by good parenting, who look beyond the confines and shackles of their demographic plight and make something of themselves. There is another old saying which goes, "You cannot take a person out of the slums. Take the slums out of the person, and then the person will take himself out of the slums."

White society may have originally put the majority of blacks into the hopelessness of slum life. But for blacks to rage that whites are still to blame is untrue and unfair. Whites have made many sacrifices to advance the liberties and success of blacks, even to the cost of many of their lives. Moreover, Welfare legislation has created programs not to free the black from the slums, but to keep him there. The best thing our government can do for their pitiable plight is to support the family and its stability. Strong families create strong individuals, who repeat the process, strengthening society thereby.

If I watch the TV news these days, half the time I am going to become depressed and agitated by racist rantings from very unhappy blacks. Whites cannot seem to do anything right in the eyes of some of these people. *I am among the first to stand up for justice for blacks* when there is clear evidence that any whites have committed brutality or crimes against them. But there is sad substantiation that the issue of race is far from being healed and resolved. Well, according to the press and the agitators.

Yet I am convinced that these angry mobs represent a minority of the black race, while for the most part they are a loving and gentle people eager to be friendly with the average white. News media portray white and black relations as a scene from a horror movie. Such is not the case in reality. Whites and blacks enjoy true friendship at unprecedented levels, and for the most part discrimination is a thing of the past. Current rebellious trends in poor neighborhoods, exploited by the news media and agitators, is unraveling decades of sterling progress made by black Americans, who to a large degree did so hand-in-hand with white supporters.

Slavery, and discrimination after it was outlawed, have dealt a cruel blow to black society in America, to be sure. But this stems from an age-old evil that has plagued humanity for millennia. It unfortunately has always existed, since ancient times, among all peoples. It was practiced every time one people conquered another, and captured their survivors for subjugation. The ancient Romans, Greeks, Egyptians, Middle Easterners, Asians—they all did it. Even England practiced enslavement of their own people in olden times. It has always been a part of life. I certainly do not excuse it on those grounds, nor on any basis. It is inherently evil, and shall always thus remain. It is of little comfort that blacks started the black slave trade in Africa, when they would sell captured people to Arab slave traders, who then sold them to the slave traders of Europe and America. All who were involved were committing evil: blacks, whites, and Arabs. Sadly, the practice continues today, though on a smaller scale, in many parts of the world. But even if only one person were subjected to slavery, it is a travesty of horrendous proportions.

With all the progress in race relations I have witnessed in my life time, I hope I also live to see it secured, and not deprecated, by the forces sad evil that tend to stir people up one against another. I have to admit that blacks have suffered horrendously in the past, even to the point of the evilest forms of violence against them. Then came the generations of psychological torture which they have endured with astounding resilience. We have managed for the most part to defuse that and leave it in the dust of the past. I pray we can continue upon the path of brotherly and sisterly love: it is there—the majority of whites and blacks enjoy an unprecedented level of friendship. Please, any unhappy blacks or complacent whites, let us come together and work this thing out. Agitators, your day is done; go home. God wants us all to be happy, and equally desires our kindness to each other; for we are all truly brothers and sisters, and one day will have to give an accounting of how we treated one another.

EPILOGUE

In looking back from whence I came, I am astounded that I lived to see this day. My life has been a sojourn sometimes of heaviness, but mostly of happiness. There are bounteous blessings from a loving Heavenly Father to enjoy. Chief among these are family and friendships. It is incumbent upon the individual to seek after and make the most of these choice blessings. I cannot speak for the entire white race; I can only speak for myself. I hope my life, though tempted and tainted in earlier years with traces of inherent racism, has nonetheless been one of truly extending the hand of love and fellowship to the black race, particularly to individuals I have met along life's highway. My Christian love toward blacks and all fellow humankind far outweighs any inherited prejudicial tendencies, the latter of which I have always striven to unravel and decompose within me. Dear reader, be merciful in your assessment of this humble writer. I hope I have done more good than harm. God help us in building bridges and not tearing them down.

"Keep the faith, baby." (Adam Clayton Powell, late pastor and Congressman from Harlem, New York City.)

ABOUT THE AUTHOR

J. B. Turner is a retired counselor, songwriter, and veteran of the Vietnam war, in which he served at age 18. He has served as a lay minister and Scout leader. His fields of study include psychology, English literature, and rehabilitation administration. His hobbies include history, genealogy, songwriting, and ancient American archeology. His love of family, the Gospel, and community are the mainstays of his life.

He strives to actively live the commandments of God and the teachings of his church, which include a sincere reaching out to all of God's children: "red and yellow, black and white, they are precious in His sight."

He composed this entire book from one small page of notes. (See illustration following.) So deep and wide are his feelings on the subject, that decades' worth of thoughts flowed continually during the writing, requiring only a few brief external notations of significant incidents he wanted to be sure to include.

ILLUSTRATIONS

ENTIRE NOTES USED FOR THIS BOOK:
(Small sheet, 5x7 inches:)

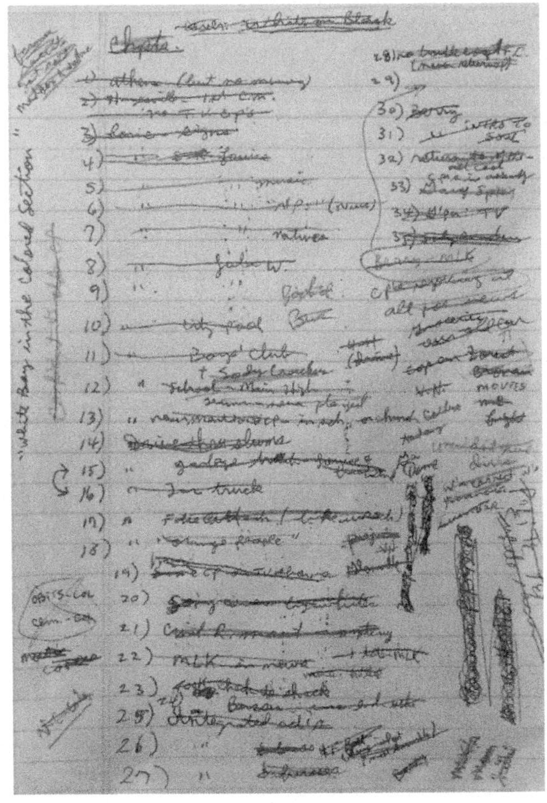

2016: A BLACK GEORGIA ATHLETE IS HONORED ON THE SIGN OF A RESTAURANT NAMED FOR A CONFEDERATE GENERAL, AND MAINLY FREQUENTED BY "GOOD OL' GEORGIA BOYS:"

A white church in the heart of South Georgia's cotton country, founded in the 1840's for the purpose of including blacks. Whites were locked out of their own church for being unprejudiced, and were willing to take steps for truer spiritual harmony. Good can prevail if we are determined:

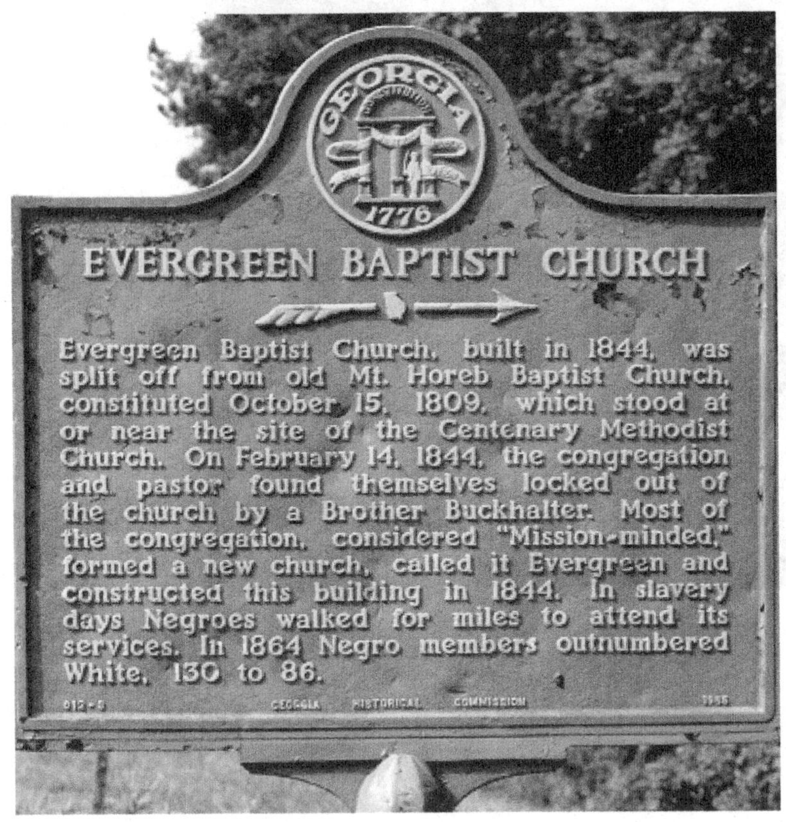

My granddaughter, 5, admires Dr. King's "I Have A Dream" speech from 1963. I was 11 when it occurred, and although it was covered by the press and most of the audience were whites, <u>I never even heard about it until I was grown.</u> It was not discussed in white circles where I lived, but it has endured, and the impact continues on and on. <u>It is now discussed regularly in the schools that had once failed to see it worthy of social consideration.</u>

Times have changed ~ friendship fills the air.
May we all reach out in kindness and dignity.

BOOKS BY J. B. TURNER:

The Phantom Of Phu Bai

High Humor Of The Hills

Blood At Alamance!
The Murder Of Innocence: A Governor's Guilt

White Boy In The Colored Section

Victim Of Valor

Made in the USA
Monee, IL
07 July 2026

56552149R00069